THE ART OF
SOARING

THE ART OF
SOARING

DOLOKHOV & GURANGOV

Translated by Mark Havill, Ph.D.
Edited by Leonid Sharashkin, Ph.D.

DEEP SNOW PRESS
Ithaca • New York

Vladimir Dolokhov and Vadim Gurangov

The Art of Soaring

Translated from the Russian by Mark Havill
Edited by Leonid Sharashkin

ISBN: 978-0-9842873-1-4

Library of Congress Control Number: 2009940492

Printed on 100% post-consumer recycled paper.

Published by Deep Snow Press

www.DeepSnowPress.com

CONTENTS

TRANSLATOR'S PREFACE

I first met Papa (Vladimir Dolokhov) in the summer of 1993 at a week-long spiritual gathering of several hundred Russians in the countryside outside of Moscow. People from all over Russia came to practice Yoga, Buddhism, Tai Chi, Healing, Dances of Universal Peace, and all manner of alternative lifestyles. It was my fifth time in Russia, but that particular summer I was doing dissertation research at the Russian Academy of Sciences in St. Petersburg, escaping the city whenever I could to attend gatherings and lead workshops in Sufi practices.

After the train ride and an hour packing in on foot, I arrived at the camp situated along the Yakhroma River. I had been to this particular gathering the previous year with my family, so already knew many Russians there. I was the only foreigner.

My first impression as I walked around the camp was of an enthusiastic crowd of people sitting in a circle around Papa, laughing uproariously as he extemporized freely and animatedly. Spiritual development through laughter has always been a trademark of his message. The mirth was infectious, so I joined them. Although at that time I had studied Russian for over thirty years, it wasn't easy for me to follow his train of thought—the subtleties of humor are difficult to translate—but enjoyed the laughter without being distracted by the meaning.

During that week Papa and I formed a deep bond of friendship through shared practices and conversation. One particularly profound connection we made happened while gathering firewood together. In his boundless energy, Papa was literally leaping about the forest, throwing logs into piles, wildly chopping them into pieces, and loading himself up with astonishing stacks of firewood to take back to camp. At one point, we stood facing each other, hands on shoulders, and just gazed into each other's eyes. An incredible presence of being flowed between us—strength, groundedness, the warrior, the lover, the healer, the fool. Those few moments of total connection felt like an eternity. Throughout the rest of that week, we shared many such moments—and, yes, much laughter, too—and have been friends and fellow travelers on the Path ever since.

I met Beard (Vadim Gurangov) much later, in the summer of 2001. He and Papa had sponsored me to come to Russia to teach a weekend workshop in Moscow. My first impression of him was of a quiet, mild-mannered man with a radiant heart. But at lunch that day in a traditional Russian restaurant (folkloric paintings and textiles on the walls, the strains of a balalaika filling the room), I found him to be a fun, hilarious person full of exuberance and life. After the workshop, several of us shared a Russian banya (sauna), lovingly thrashing each other with veniki (bunches of birch twigs) in the burning hot steam, cooling off in the icy pool, and, as always, laughing. Beard was usually at the center of joy wherever it bubbled up from our overflowing hearts.

In this book the authors present a uniquely Russian system for developing one's inner potential and improving conditions in life. The fundamental principle is an understanding of the interconnection between the inner and outer worlds. Outer circumstances are reflections of our inner state, and by changing ourselves on the inside—the way we perceive and understand the world—we can positively alter the conditions of our outer lives. All is performed in the spirit of joy, laughter, and play, even to the point of absurdity.

The first part of the book explains their basic premises, sometimes directly, oftentimes humorously, and everywhere interwoven with the adventures of a folk hero on a symbolic quest through the inner realms. This section provides a basic theoretical understanding of their system.

The second part of the book narrates the personal stories of people who have been helped by their techniques. These stories tell of physical, mental, and emotional healing, and how people have used this system to dramatically change their lives, attaining what they want in life both inwardly and outwardly.

The entire book is liberally sprinkled with quotes from various Russian authors and mystics, as well as from Westerners ranging from Lewis Carroll to Richard Bach to Carlos Castaneda.

It has been my great pleasure to translate this book which has helped so many people sort out the difficult issues of their lives. I have learned much in the process, finally understanding the subtleties of their system beyond the joyful laughter and playful games.

"Thank you, Vanya, for letting me see that without the joy of life I might descend into a morose state of seriousness, with no friends around me, and only the drudgery of life to drag me along through a cold, heartless existence."

"I am the one who gathers firewood with Papa!"

"I am the one who steams in the hot banya with Beard!"

In gratitude, I offer to both Beard and Papa the gift of a winged salmon soaring off into a pastel-tinted sunrise attended by golden dragon flies, brightly reflecting the sun, zipping merrily around it.

May this book give you, too, the tools to improve the conditions of your life, to become whole and self-confident, to truly love, and to lighten your heart with joy and laughter.

Mark Havill, Ph.D.
Translator

About the Translator

Mark Havill, Ph.D., has studied Russian for nearly fifty years, culminating in his Ph.D. in Slavic Linguistics and Folklore from the University of Virginia. Since 1987 he has traveled to Russia 15 times, teaching workshops in cities and at summer gatherings in the country. He has practiced conscious spiritual development for over 35 years and is a Sheikh in the Sufi Ruhaniat International. He has known and worked with the authors since 1993.

INTRODUCTION

Neznaika peered suspiciously at the old man:
"Perhaps you're also going to tell me that you are the magician!"
"Yes, I *am* the magician."

Nikolay Nosov—Neznaika in Sun City

When we set out to write this introduction, we decided to consider our own experience of purchasing books. First, you look at the title. If it appeals to you, you may read the back cover and table of contents. This may compel you to quickly thumb through the book. If the passages you chance to read catch your interest, and you are in general agreement with the author's viewpoint, then you may finally decide to buy the book. You probably won't even glance at the introduction until you've arrived home, or perhaps along the way. We recommend that, when buying this book, you use this strategy.

This introduction is dedicated to all those who read introductions.

Little Nikita, with trembling heart, kept glancing up at the clock. It was less than an hour before midnight on New Year's Eve. He was on the floor playing with his toys, but his thoughts were far away. He was picturing Grandfather Frost with a huge sack of gifts, one of which was surely the Sony PlayStation which he wanted more than anything else in the world. However, a shadow of doubt clouded this cheer-ful scene: "What if Grandfather Frost mixes up the gifts?" Nikita tried to comfort himself by remembering that last year Grandfather Frost had not messed up at all, giving him the toy robot he had so anxiously hoped for. Gradually, these thoughts lulled him into sleep. When he awoke the next morning, Nikita, burning with curiosity, dashed straight for the tree…

Is this scene familiar to you? Everyone believes in mir-acles, regardless of whether you are aware of it or not. The expectation of miracles is especially strong among children. A child lives in fairytales. He plays and converses with fairytale characters—Snow White, the Baba Yaga witch, Karlsson-on-the-Roof. He sincerely believes that magicians really do exist, even that he is one himself. As he grows up, however, the world gradually becomes more and more predictable; there is no longer any place for miracles. But these childhood memo-ries still flicker deep in the heart of every person, and they can unexpectedly rise to the surface at any time.

From earliest times, Russians have been characterized as quick-witted, irrationally hopeful, and naturally lazy. We are raised on fairy tales, whose heroes are often ingenious loafers. Emelia the Fool, lounging on the stove, has his every wish granted with the simple spell: "By the will of the Pike, do as I like." While drinking in a tavern, Ivanushka, also a fool, manages to catch the humpbacked horse Konyok-Gorbunok and with its help seizes the Tsar's throne, winning the hand of Elena the Beautiful. The quick-witted and nimble cat, Kotofey Ivanych, hardly lifting a paw, becomes king of the forest animals and lives out his life in luxury.

The ability to act the fool and, not troubling yourself too overly much, to receive instantly all that you desire is a unique peculiarity of our national character. This is attested to even by the names of the heroes in fairytales—for example, Kuzma Skorobogaty, which means "Kuzma Quickrich." Irrational hope* is vividly portrayed in the tale *The Flying Ship*. An old man asks the fool:

"Do you know how to build a flying ship, so you can win the princess's hand in marriage?"

"No, not really."

"Then why are you going?"

"I haven't the slightest. Things just seem to work out!"

And, you know, it did work out well for him!

The world around us is mysterious and unpredictable; it is not always possible to squeeze it all into the Procrustean bed of our limited personal projects. However many plans we make, it is impossible to foresee everything, all the more so in an enigmatic society like Russia with its never-ending series of "surprises"—perestroika, the putsch, the Dry Law, the 17th of August,** and so on.

The unorthodox actions of fairytale heroes, their unusual behavior, often lead to fantastic rewards. In the tale *The Magic Ring*, Martynka, in reward for successfully completing a task, was given the choice between a bag of sand and a bag of silver. It is not difficult to guess that Martynka chose the bag of sand, which turned out to contain a magic ring which would grant any wish. When our plans are neither limited by

---

* Russian: *avos'*—literally, "the axis of Creation." Reliance on *avos'*, while irrational, is not unintelligent. Rather, it is based on the intuitive understanding of the order of the Universe. [trans]

** 17th of August, 1998—on that date, the Russian government defaulted on servicing many of its debt obligations. As a result, the Russian ruble lost 80% of its value almost overnight, numerous banks collapsed, and many Russians lost their life savings. [trans]

a particular concrete result, nor do they depend on a reasonable amount of time to attain it, then the possible result will often exceed our wildest expectations.

The methods used in fairy tales to achieve results are extraordinarily simple. The ritual to materialize the flying ship, from the tale of the same name, is a masterpiece of fairytale magic:

"Walk up to the first tree you see, cross yourself three times, and strike it with an ax. Then fall to the ground face down and go to sleep. When you wake up, you will see the ship before you ready to go."

Foolish behavior, a belief in miracles, the habit of getting what they want "without coming down from the stove," and the sense of humor typical of these charming heroes of Russian folktales are the foundation of magical art as set forth in this book.

Over the years we, too, had ceased believing in miracles. But then miracles again came into our lives. In fact, they began occurring daily.

Reading standard esoteric literature may give the impression that magic can only be carried out with the help of objects of power, or by performing magical rites or spells. In our view, these are all secondary. The most important aspect of magic is that special state of being when you are charged with energy. In shamanism this state is reached by entering into a trance, often achieved through ritual dance and playing musical instruments like tambourines, drums, didgeridoos, flutes... Sometimes certain psychotropic substances are also utilized.

In traditional magic this state can be attained by observing a multitude of mysterious and unintelligible actions (rituals), whose details must be performed with strict exactness; any deviation could put the magician in mortal peril. As a rule, rituals are accompanied by ancient and powerful incantations secretly passed down by word of mouth from master to student.

In this book we propose a humorous, light-hearted approach to magic based on an extraordinary state of being we call *soaring*. Entry into this state occurs by various means—for example, by exaggerating problematic situations to outcomes which stretch the limits of absurdity, which cause the magician to laugh uproariously, or at least to smile, enabling the drama and seriousness of the issue to just fall away. It all becomes comical, and an unusual and creative way of embodying magic in life is revealed.

The principle foundation of our approach requires a healthy sense of humor, boldness of thought and action—perhaps a child's game—and sometimes even a bit of mischief. Magic is no longer a complex science full of peril, but instead it becomes light, harmless, and fully accessible to all.

Acknowledgments

We are thankful to Josefina, who brought to our attention many mistakes and inaccuracies in the manuscript. Then Nina, Zhanna, and Alexandra read through the manuscript and suggested many useful changes. Finally, Lucia accomplished the monumental task of proofreading the manuscript. In the interests of future readers, she helped us simplify the text significantly and to clarify several obscure passages. We could never have dreamed of having such excellent editors. We offer to all of them our sincerest appreciation.

Special thanks also go to N. A. Morozov (populist), M. M. Postnikov, Evgeny Shchepin, Yuri Muranov, Nadya Zhavko, Sasha Fedorov, Andrey Khudiyarov, Nikolay Kurilkin, Slava Tabachenko, Vasily Ivanych Chapaev, Victor Pelevin and Baron Yungern, Old Man Khottabych, don Jenaro, don Juan, and don Carlos, the Yakhroma River, Summer Solstice Gatherings, Vasudeva and Big White Nastya, the Dances of Universal Peace and Samuel Lewis, Milton Erickson, Richard Bandler and John Grinder, Roger Zelazny and Robert Heinlein, Granny Dundusa from the village Nizhnie Varguny, Russian fairy tales, Hawaiian shamans, Donald Shimoda and Richard Bach, our wives Lenulia and Lucia, Lao Tzu, Krishnamurti, the Pentium-133, the Hewlett Packard LaserJet 6L, Microsoft, the electronics store "Mitinsky Radiorynok," the films *Back to the Future* and *Nebyvalshchina*,* and the musical group "Enigma."

---

* *Nebyvalshchina*—a 1983 Soviet film directed by Sergey Ovcharov. Grounded in Russian folklore, this film is full of surreal scenes of "what cannot be," such as peasants plowing the snow or a blacksmith forging young maidens out of old hags. [trans]

SOME THEORY
FOR THE CURIOUS

For in and out, above, about, below,
'Tis nothing but a Magic Shadow-show,
Play'd in a Box whose Candle is the Sun,
Round which we Phantom Figures come and go.
Omar Khayyam—Rubaiyat

Imagine yourself in a crowded, stuffy room. Everywhere people are sitting on old, dilapidated chairs, on rickety stools, on packs—wherever they can. Some who are quick try to occupy two chairs at the same time, or to snatch seats away from others. This is like the world we live in. But at the same time, each of us also possesses our own personal throne, enormous, magnificent, rising high above everything in this world, even above everything in all other worlds. This throne is truly grand and majestic. Nothing is impossible for the person who ascends to it, and, even more important, it is wholly legitimate. It is the lawful right of each person. But to ascend this throne is nearly impossible, since it stands in a place which does not exist... It is nowhere.
Victor Pelevin—*Chapaev and Emptiness*

THE ART OF SOARING

Suddenly it dawned on him:
"Wait!" he shouted. "That was flying! We were flying!"
The Hermit nodded.
"I know," he said. "The truth is simpler
than you can imagine."
                    Victor Pelevin—*Hermit and Six-Toes*

Have you ever watched how a bird soars on the wind? How
it spreads its wings and glides easily through the air? Nothing
hinders its flight. Merging with the elements, it becomes one
with them. It flies effortlessly, sailing endlessly through the
blue sky.

Soaring is one of the principal concepts of the system for
practical magic described in this book. It is exceedingly difficult to describe this state of soaring in words, because it is
a subjective inner experience for each person. While soaring,
it never even enters your mind to attempt to name or define
what you are feeling, and the circumstances of life which en-
able one person to soar may mean nothing to another. Only
through metaphor is it possible to express this feeling, as in
the following story.

When I was a young boy, I learned to ride a bicycle.
At first it was very difficult to maintain my balance. Each
time I started out, my bicycle, seemingly bewitched, again

and again toppled over, and I crashed down hard onto the pavement, scratched and bruised.

At last, though, I finally managed to "catch" that feeling of balance and, desperately swerving from side to side, I set off. Gradually I was able to steady myself and felt my dark blue "Mustang" become subservient to my will. I merged with the bicycle and, peddling effortlessly, I rode forward. The entire world around me—the gray pavement of the street and the long shadows of the setting sun, the lilac bushes and the hollow old pear tree, the chirping of the birds and the gentle summer breeze—everything took on an altered and elusive meaning. I can't explain this feeling, but in this new world my every wish was granted. Each moment was unique and absorbed me entirely.

You can sink into a very powerful state of soaring through spiritual dance (Dances of Universal Peace). Following is a brief description of the authors' impressions of one such evening of dancing.

Taking hands and forming a large circle, we sing an intricate song in an ancient language, accompanied by guitar and drum. With quickening tempo, our feet trace the beautiful pattern of the "grapevine step." Each person moves in syncopation with two other dancers—the partner and corner— first facing one, then the other. In the second part of the dance, the dancers, whirling rapidly, exchange places with their partner, face a new partner, and the dance is begun anew.

Combining a song in a powerful, ancient language with beautiful movements of the body, as joyful faces flash constantly before your eyes, brings you into a state of soaring. An energy of amazing force swirls around the hall. The eyes of the dancers sparkle brightly, smiles shine on faces, and the atmosphere is electrified by a powerful discharge of happiness and universal love. The mood and strength of purpose fills each dancer with ecstasy.

An exuberant Russian dance "Oy, How Good It Is!" is the highlight of the program; we dance it with wild abandon. It is interesting to observe the beginners—how their faces are gradually changing, how their eyes begin to shine with love and joy.

An especially deep state of consciousness is reached when we do a slow, meditative dance. Singing a simple melody, we move to a slow and easy rhythm, bowing slightly to the right, to the left, rocking forward and backward, like rowing a boat, sinking gradually into vast depths of inner bliss.

We feel a warm glow in the center of our breast; a gentle, pleasant fire flares up within us, crackling steadily like birch logs blazing in a well-stoked Russian woodstove. Our hearts expand to encompass the entire hall, merging with the other dancers, pulsating in time with the movements, the singing.

We become one with the circle; we are both the observer and the observed; everyone sings through us, and we sing through everyone. Who is it that moves us? Who sings with our voice? Where have space and time disappeared to? These questions hang in the atmosphere.

The evening ends with a heartfelt dance from the East, in which partners gaze deeply into each other's eyes. And the finale of this miracle-play—sweet hugging. We hug in silence, merging with each partner in the One Breath. Long after the dance, we remain in this state of soaring, and the whole world dances with us.

Even after the dances are over, it is still easy to enter into this state of soaring—you just remember the words or the melody of a dance, the eyes of your partners, or simply recall the warmth glowing in your heart.

Throughout our lives each of us has such experiences of soaring—when we learn to walk, to swim, to dance, to paint...

Soaring arouses a person to create, inspiration flows, every contact with this new world produces perfect works of art, whether this manifests as a drawing or a cake recipe, composing a song or building a house, or as a scientific discovery... We often experience soaring in our dreams—while flying, writing poetry, finding lost objects, solving complex scientific equations...

We hope that you, too, can remember such experiences of soaring in your own life.

WORLD VIEW

"Oh, you can't help that," said the Cat. "We're all mad here. I'm mad. You're mad."

"How do you know I'm mad?" said Alice.

"You must be," said the Cat, "or you wouldn't have come here."

Lewis Carroll—Alice's Adventures in Wonderland

Reality is imaginary, and the imaginary is real!

Vseslav Solo—The Fundamentals of Magic

The world in which we live is a group visualization, which we have been taught to uphold from the day of our birth. In fact, this is really the only thing which one generation passes to another.

Victor Pelevin—Chapaev and Emptiness
(a.k.a. Buddha's Little Finger)

What we call the physical universe is actually based on agreement. The atom, for example, is simply an agreement among physicists. Now they have come to an agreement on the existence of an even greater number of smaller particles which they cannot even see.

Luke Rhinehart —Transformation

It is impossible to comprehend the incomprehensible.

Kozma Prutkov

For the past several years, we have attempted to comprehend the laws of the universe, the mechanism of cause and effect, in order to better understand the world we live in. A person— more exactly, the mind—constantly tries to explain what is happening in life: Why some things happen to us, but other things don't work out; why we encounter particular people at a particular time; why some people are loved while others are despised or ignored; why some people are rich while others are poor; some are healthy, but others are ailing.*

We have attempted to discover the answers to these questions in erudite books on esotericism and psychology, and at seminars addressing these themes.

We began our search for truth by practicing Yoga, and therefore fanatically believed in "energy," "chakras," and "Kundalini." We became strict vegetarians, regularly cleansing our organisms of accumulated toxins and, to conserve our sexual energy, we consciously directed it toward spiritual development.

During this time, we pored over many esoteric books and were greatly impressed by the works of Carlos Castaneda and Richard Bach, both of whom still influence us today. In our view, the principal concept in the works of Castaneda is becoming aware of your "description of the world" (we prefer the term "world view")—your perception of the universe which you begin forming at birth (perhaps even at conception), and which is constantly affirmed by an unspoken agreement with the people around you. We call this mutually accepted agreement the *common world view*.

---

* Usually we search for reasons for events which affect us when life's circumstances are unfavorable (i.e., not as we wish them to be). Instead of dwelling on our misfortune, this book proposes a system which uses magical techniques to alter life's circumstances in a favorable direction.

Actually, the common world view is like a religion, whose dogma is rarely discussed; its adherents (most people) are like religious fanatics who unquestioningly believe that it is the one and only truth. Many people fear falling under the influence of some obscure cult, of which there are so many these days (also a component of the common world view). They do not realize that, in fact, they have already belonged to a cult for their entire lives—the religious cult professed by the common world view. Figuratively speaking, each person through the course of a day (and for most even in the night) are constantly intoning prayers like this: "I believe in the regular alternation of day and night, and of the seasons. I believe that people exist and that I am a person, that I have one head, one body, two arms, two legs, and that I belong to a specific gender (not all believe this last part). I believe in the power of money and bow down to its supreme authority. I believe that the earth is round and that it rotates around the sun. I believe in the Law of Gravity. I believe that I will die… In the name of Space, Time, and Matter, Amen!"

"This isn't a matter of faith!" you might exclaim. "It's just speaking the obvious. You can see proof of the laws of nature (i.e., dogmas) anywhere you look; there are no exceptions. And I can prove that I'm right. What if I whacked you over the head with a stick? Then I'd like to hear what you have to say about life being an illusion!"

By all means, we do not want to stick out our necks by challenging the common world view; in fact, we, too, profess it.

"Come on! Even to propose that the common world view is an illusion is some crazy pipe dream!"

It was the writer Richard Bach who profoundly influenced us with ideas about the illusoriness of the world. However, the first strike against the "real world" was inflicted by the works of the great Russian scientist and populist, Nikolay Morozov—*Revelation in Thunder and Storm*, *The Prophets*, and a series of seven books under the general name of *The Christ*. His works convincingly prove that modern perceptions of ancient history are little more than myth, collections of "historical novels."

Morozov critiques classical views of history, applying data from astronomy, geophysics, paleontology, philology, and many other sciences to support his conclusions. The established historical world view collapses under the onslaught of data he presents from the natural sciences. Not only did Morozov overthrow the classical historical world view, but he also constructed a new way of viewing history out of the wreckage of the old.

A talented man with a rich imagination, he *singlehandedly* constructed this alternate historical world view, while it took the efforts of thousands of scholars to construct the common world view. Morozov's historical world view is stunning! Here are some of the ideas he proposes: the antiquity of the Eastern cultures in India and China is greatly overstated; they appeared in the Middle Ages, later than ancient Rome. Also, Classical Antiquity and the Renaissance were of the same epoch, and, consequently, the "Dark Ages" did not separate them. Ancient Egypt was part of the Roman Empire, and the pharaohs were actually Roman emperors. The Mongol and Tartar invasions of Rus' did not occur, and, in fact, the Mongol and Tartar Khans were Russian princes who had lost in the battle for power taking place in Russia at that time.*

After reading through the works of Morozov, we began to suspect that, in fact, neither the classical historical world view nor Morozov's alternate view truly describes "real history." Most likely, "real history" simply does not exist! Moreover, the common historical view is a direct reflection of the illusion promulgated by the common world view which most people adhere to.

Let's consider how we create our world, more exactly, our common world view.** Suppose that at birth we know nothing, our minds are a "blank slate." We not only don't know that the world is round, but we don't even suspect that the world exists at all. Furthermore, we are completely unaware of physical boundaries, and that we have a body—two arms, two legs, a head, etc. In our mother's womb we perceived the world as a single, complete whole, not divided into separate parts, and we fully identified with this world (the womb).

From immemorial times there has existed a legend in human society, which was never open to question. It states that women only give birth to beings with *human form*, not a baby crocodile or some other kind of wild beast. An expecting mother, naturally, believes in this legend.

While the fetus is developing in the womb, the mother imagines how her newborn baby will look, and if it stirs faintly within her, she "knows" exactly which "part of the body" it is moving. Relatives and friends of the expecting mother are also convinced that she is bearing a small human being. In

---

* Morozov's works on Russian history were never published, but are stored in the archives of the Russian Academy of Sciences. Currently, Morozov's historical world view is being further developed by a group of scientists under the leadership of academician A. T. Fomenko, who is not a professional historian but rather a mathematician. After two decades (grade school, college, graduate school) of buying into the common historical world view, it has been exceedingly difficult to renounce it.

** This is very beautifully and plausibly expressed in a short story by Victor Pelevin "Ivan Kublakhanov."

this way, the people surrounding the child begin to define its features even while in the womb—*they actually help form its physical body*, training it to be an individual being separated off from the rest of the world. The culmination of this process is the moment of birth. The infant, in fact similar to a human being, is inspected by the obstetricians. They touch and probe various parts of its body; they swaddle it. Over time, constant conditioning helps solidify the image of the human form.

"Where are baby's cute little eyes? Now show me mommy's eyes. Here are the doll's eyes... Look: stick, stick, little cucumber—here's the baby!"

While still in the womb, a most important concept begins to take root in the world of the unborn child—*time*. From the moment of conception, two rhythms are constantly present to the fetus—coming from somewhere unknown, it hears the regular beating of a huge metronome (the mother's heart), and its universe continuously expands and contracts with a steady rhythm (the mother's breathing). The child's universe operates according to set routines—during the "night" it rests, during the "day" it is active, etc. Routines continue after birth as well, such as feedings given at strictly determined times.

Next, influenced by its surroundings, the child begins the process of *constructing* various objects in its world. Out of the surrounding chaos, a newborn is taught how to identify people, objects, plants, animals, etc., assigning to each concept concrete, recognizable features. The young child is shown some kind of indistinct blur and hears "Mama, mama, mama...," and gradually the child learns to construct "mama." You might say that, metaphorically, each word names a *slide* collection stored in the memory. For example, behind the word "chair" stand all the images of chairs which the child has seen in its brief existence. In this way, the particular *language* it learns becomes its most important *instrument for creating reality*.

As the child confidently begins to distinguish (material-ize) objects, he learns to link a series of different images into an uninterrupted sequence, filling in absent interrelationships between frames. The internal slides "come to life" and turn into *internal movies*, which have sound, smell, kinetic sensa-tion, etc. He starts understanding entire sentences, represent-ed by the name of the corresponding movie—for example "Mama is cooking oatmeal." At this point, the *law of cause and effect* is introduced:

"Don't touch the stove, or you'll burn your fingers; eat your oatmeal, and I'll give you a treat…"

Figuratively speaking, each person, while growing up, be-comes a storehouse for these internal movies (as Gurdjieff expresses it, turning into a "mechanical person"). The primary movies are created early on, and whenever new information is received from the surrounding world, the child translates it into words, instantly editing its internal movie from available film clips and slides.

The sum total of all these internal movies becomes the person's *world view.**

Furthermore, each person's world view is unique to him-self or herself, personal. In fact, during social interactions we only give the appearance that we truly understand each other. When we talk to another person, we can only describe our own world view, which may be drastically different from that of the other person.

The world view of a European and a bushman is strikingly different. This is brilliantly portrayed in the film *The Gods Must Be Crazy*. As shown in the film, a bushman perceives a truck as a huge, fast-running wild beast with a head, paws, ears, and tail.

* Instead of "world view," it may be more exact to use the phrase "film library," but we will stick to the generally accepted term.

Similarly, the world view of a person who has lost his mind differs just as strikingly from the world view of "normal" people.

How are new objects constructed in the mind? A mental patient in the film *Twelve Monkeys* superbly explains the discovery of microbes in this monologue:

> *You know what "crazy" is? "Crazy" is "majority. rules." Take germs, for example. In the 18th century, there was no such thing! Nobody had ever imagined such a thing—no sane person anyway. Along comes this doctor... Samuel Weiss, I think. He tries to convince people, other doctors mostly, that there are these teeny tiny, invisible "bad things" called germs that get into your body and make you... sick! He's trying to get doctors to wash their hands.*
>
> *So cut to the 20th century! Last week, in fact, right before I got dragged into this hellhole. I order a burger in this fast food joint. The waiter drops it on the floor. He picks it up, wipes it off, hands it to me... like it was all okay. "What about the germs?" I say. He goes: "I don't believe in germs. Germs are just a plot they made up so they can sell you disinfectants and soap!"*
>
> *Now, he's crazy, right? Hey, you believe in germs, don't you? There's only "majority rules." There is no right, no wrong... Only what everyone thinks is true.*

We would add that the further materialization of microbes followed as would be expected—scientists saw them in microscopes, discovered new types, classified them, etc.

In a similar way, the AIDS virus was created not long ago. The process is described in detail by James P. Hogan in the chapter "AIDS Heresy and the New Bishops" of his book *Rockets, Redheads and Revolution.**

Citing the research of Peter Duesberg, professor of molecular and cellular biology at the University of California, Berkeley, Hogan presents a convincing argument that AIDS in reality does not exist, that the entire epidemic has been created out of thin air for profit. We will briefly cite here a few of his conclusions.

At the end of the 1980's, Duesberg published an article stating that AIDS could not possibly have arisen from HIV—in fact, from any kind of virus at all. Duesberg performed a detailed analysis of the correspondence between AIDS and four criteria for infectious diseases known as Koch's Postulates. He ascertained that, regarding the theory that HIV causes AIDS, not one of these criteria were fulfilled—i.e., AIDS is not infectious!

He believes that the reason for inventing AIDS is obvious.

While searching for a cure for polio in the beginning of the 1960's, American medical research institutions graduated a large number of virologists. When this task was finally completed, all the human and institutional resources which had been required for the polio epidemic began seeking another crusade to embark on—to discover a cure for the "new deadly virus" and to produce a vaccine to combat it. Federal expenditures grew annually to billions of dollars. Never before had the scientific-medical establishment and the bureaucrats managing it received such a generous largesse.

Serving the victims of AIDS was funded at the public expense, which meant lucrative consultation fees, costly testing, and medical procedures involving the most expensive drugs. Researchers, who otherwise would have spent their

* Hogan, James P. *Rockets, Redheads and Revolution*. Riverdale NY: Baen Books, 1999.

lives peering into microscopes and washing out Petri dishes, became millionaires by founding companies to manufacture HIV testing equipment and materials, and to charge patients money for performing the tests.

For his attacks against this "Golden Calf," Duesberg—a pioneer in researching retroviruses, recipient of a seven-year Outstanding Investigator Grant from the National Institutes of Health, and candidate for the Nobel Prize for his work in discovering oncogenes—was greeted by howls of abuse and scorn, his theories discredited, and his research grants sharply reduced.

You may ask: "Even if we do grant that AIDS was, indeed, invented, people are still dying from it."

Duesberg maintains that they are dying not from AIDS but rather from a range of diseases connected with immunodeficiency: pneumonia, tuberculosis, various infections, etc. However, our feeling is that they are, in fact, dying from the common world view, which considers AIDS to be an incurable disease. All world views reside in the mind, and when a person focuses on a particular issue, his imagination bestows it with life, and the accepted model becomes active.

Hogan has painted quite an impressive picture of the world! No wonder physicians have so strenuously sought out ever new and more terrible diseases, and the mass media continues to diligently report their discoveries. Fortunately, they have not yet been able to achieve global acceptance for a new replacement for AIDS.

The principal method by which new objects are introduced into the common world view is simple. A person with a rich imagination creates a movie which did not previously exist. As long as the movie lives only in the consciousness of a single "madman," it is dangerous to proclaim the new discovery to the world; they will just send him to the nuthouse. In order for a newly invented phenomenon to be accepted as real, you have to convince everyone around you that it does indeed exist. Actually, you only have to convince a small group of authoritative people—scientists, politicians, the mass media—and it is as good as done. The delusion becomes public property, a component of the mass hallucination. This model has been persuasively described in the fantasy novel by Colin Wilson *The Mind Parasites*.

The authority to construct new formations in the modern, civilized world is entrusted mainly to scientists (the high priests of the religion which professes the common world view). Consider the experience of Dmitry Ivanovich Mendeleev, who in a dream saw a rectangular table with cells containing the known chemical elements. Many of the cells, however, were still empty, but these were to be later filled in by as yet undiscovered elements, whose qualities were derived from their position in the table. No sooner had the world finished applauding his genius than these new elements began to be discovered, popping up like mushrooms after a spring shower. But what if Mendeleev had dreamed up a table in the shape of a doughnut? Or if he had attempted to construct his classification in three dimensions?

We can only imagine how many great discoveries and inventions are buried in the back rooms of psycho wards!

Not long ago, we were on our way to a distant city to present a workshop. The radio in the train compartment was turned on, and the announcer was saying:

"Physicists from Dubna Research Center near Moscow have succeeded in synthesizing a new 114th element on the Periodic Table of Mendeleev. They report that it remained in existence for a full 30(!) seconds. This is a great discovery, inasmuch as previous newly discovered elements have lasted for only microseconds(!!).”

This requires no commentary.

“Aha!” an astute reader might exclaim. “From what you say, all our troubles come out of the common world view! In that case, we may as well just gather up all the books of the world and burn them! To think that they even invented AIDS!”

If no one shares your world view, and it is fundamentally different from the common view, then you will be proclaimed insane, and they will isolate you from all the other lunatics who are deluded by the common world view. Therefore, you can reject the common world view, yet you must still remember its basic tenets.

If you eliminate the common world view, then you will have to invent a new collective illusion. This is not an easy task, since it is something which can only be achieved by civilization as a whole.

THOUGHT IS MATERIAL

Once while passing through a city,
I saw no people anywhere.
On every building, every house,
Were only mirrors everywhere.

If I smiled cheerfully,
The city smiled back at me;
And if I greeted anyone,
That person also greeted me.

At times the city seemed alive,
With people all around me.
Now I know I'm all alone,
And only mirrors surround me.

Andrey Makarevich—The Crystal City

"What *is* the matter?" she said, as soon as there was a chance of making herself heard. "Have you pricked your finger?"

"I haven't pricked it *yet*," the Queen said, "but I soon shall—oh, oh, oh!"

"When do you expect to do it?" Alice asked, feeling very much inclined to laugh.

"When I fasten my shawl again," the poor Queen groaned out. "The brooch will come undone directly. Oh!

Oh!" As she said the words the brooch flew open, and the
Queen clutched wildly at it, and tried to clasp it again.
    "Take care!" cried Alice. "You're holding it all crooked!"
And she caught at the brooch; but it was too late: the
pin had slipped, and the Queen had pricked her finger.
            Lewis Carroll—*Alice through the Looking Glass*

This book utilizes popular theory on thought materialization.
In our world view, this means that internal movies can be
materialized. To demonstrate this theory, we will trace the
development of two scenarios.*

    I was sitting at the computer, typing. The radio was on, and
the broadcaster announced that David Copperfield had just
publicly confessed.**
    I thought: "I've always known that he's an illusionist, pre-
tending to do real magic. I wonder how much they paid him
for his confession? People are so greedy these days."
    Suddenly, I heard a scuffle and loud cussing outside my
window.
    "And uncultured, too! Why can't they just smash in each
other's faces without all the cussing? Times are hard, and
people are pissed off! Prices have skyrocketed. If this goes on,
I won't have enough money to even feed my family."

---

* The concept of thought materialization is frequently encountered
in psychotherapy—particularly, in neuro-linguistic programming. In
psychology, it is believed that thoughts influence a person's emotions
and feelings. We would go further to say that "external reality" itself is
created by one's thoughts and emotions.

** We made this up. So much as we know, Copperfield has never confessed.

At that point, I heard a key slip into the keyhole.

"Oh, no! My wife! And I forgot to go to the store. I'm in trouble now!"

My wife gave me quite a dressing down, shouting about how she was exhausted from work, and not only had I forgotten to go to the store, but I hadn't fed the kid either.

"Things aren't right here!" I thought. "How come the man is supposed to go shopping, cook, wash the dishes, clean up, and do the laundry?"

These sullen thoughts swirled around my mind that night, keeping me awake until the early morning. I woke up with a horrendous headache...

These events could have unfolded in a different scenario. Hearing the broadcast about Copperfield, I could have responded by thinking:

"In a way, everyone's an illusionist. And if he managed all that time to pull the wool over people's eyes (like the Great Houdini), and no one could see through his tricks, then all power to him. Certainly many people, if even for a few moments, truly believed that he was flying. Sing praise to the great illusionists!"

I heard this song on the radio:

All guile, deceit has flown away,
No sham left to be seen,
Illusion's face is blown away
And smashed to smithereens.

But still I wish in my heart an' all
To save from such extremes
At least a tiny particle
Of all my rosy dreams.

Over rosy fragments tumbling,
I dance barefoot all around
I'm not in the least bit grumbling
That my hope's turned upside down.*

"Good song! I wish someone from our group would sing such a song about magicians."

Then, by the way my wife slipped the key into the keyhole, I knew immediately that she was in a great mood. And so it was—my better half was trying on the dress she'd purchased and asked me how it looked on her.

"Yes, my wife's amazing—it doesn't take much to put her in a good mood."

She cooked us a delicious dinner, and we shared a wonderful evening together. The next morning a brilliant idea came to me...

We have looked at two different scenarios in which thoughts influenced the progression of events. In the first, while listening to the broadcast about Copperfield, I immediately started playing my internal movie about bourgeois greed, which was projected into the scuffle and loud cussing; and this, in its turn, aroused feelings about future difficulties awaiting me...

These two scenarios, which here were greatly simplified, demonstrate how events could possibly unfold—either "negatively" or "positively." Usually switching between scenarios occurs chaotically, and so life's successes are "mixed," as expressed in the popular song: "After joy will come sorrow—and who knows what tomorrow."

* This song was translated by John Woodsworth. [trans]

This example shows that what's important isn't the message we receive from the outer world, but rather our *response* to it. The message is neither "good" nor "bad"— I am the one who evaluates it, who attaches to it a particular emotional coloring.

Inasmuch as thought is material, it is evident that each moment of my life *I create my own world*. Everything around me is an extension of myself, the materialization of my personal world view.

MINDFULNESS

I do not weep, I do not cry.
Just ask me, friend, I will not lie.
All life's a game, and who's to blame?
I love this life, I'm glad I came!
> Song of Ostap Bender—*The Twelve Chairs*
> (as sung by Andrey Mironov)

You walk into the theater: there's going to be battles and excitement, winners and losers, romance, disaster; you know that's all going to be there.

We buy tickets to these films, paying admission by agreeing to believe in the reality of space and the reality of time... Neither one is true, but anyone who doesn't want to pay that price cannot appear on this planet, or in any space-time system at all.
> Richard Bach—*Illusions*

You like to play when you know you can't lose, don't you?... An all-knowing expression of perfect Life has to reject all-knowingness and claim five senses only...

Do you think you're invited to play with the rest of us when you don't follow our rules? Who do you think is going to play with you?
> Richard Bach—*Running from Safety*

We offer here yet another possible world view. Let's pretend that *we really are all immortal, all-powerful beings—magicians.*

This raises the question: What do immortal beings do? How could they possibly fill all that time? The answer is— they amuse themselves... And how do they do that? With *games*, of course!

Once Papa* asked his nine-year-old son Nikita a question: "What do you think? Why are we here in this world?"

The computer gamer's answer was lightening quick: "To while away time."

To an immortal being, all that's left to do is to pleasantly pass the time, to play. A favorite game might be to totally forget your immortality and to play the mortality game of life and death. Truly, this is a most amazing game—full of surprise, success, and disappointment, pleasure and suffering, and, of course, with an unpredictable ending. "Game over!" and then what?

Imagine that we really are immortal magicians, who, having created this world, now just want to amuse ourselves, to play this mortality game within the confines of the common world view. In order to make the game more interesting, we forget about our magical abilities and *begin identifying with the players.*

What do you think? Why do some women love soap operas so passionately? Or read romance novels? Or cry all the way through a Bollywood movie? Why do men bellow, shout, and whistle at a soccer game? And when someone makes a shot for the goal, they all involuntarily kick out with their leg. The answer is obvious—women identify with heroines; they live through them. But men identify with the players.

---

* Beard and Papa are the authors' nicknames. [trans]

And how is the soap opera discussed? "Well, *I* would never have allowed Louis Albert even onto my doorstep!"

Here is another example. A child is playing on the computer for several hours, then suddenly bursts into tears: "I've been playing this game for so long and finally reached the seventh level! And then *I got killed*!"

But with grown-ups, when they get virtually "killed" or their favorite team allows (or scores) a goal, they'll up and die of a heart attack, collapsing right down onto the keyboard, or in front of the television.

We offer up the metaphor elucidated by Sergey Lukianenko in his fantasy novel *The Maze of Reflections*. The novel's hero writes an exceptional program, which allows anyone with a computer to enter a virtual world. The images on the screen become the player's actual experience. Gradually, he becomes deeply submerged into the virtual Depths—as a soldier, for example, he learns that cartridge-cases are hot, and that the recoil from a grenade launcher can knock you off your feet. He soon forgets that everything around him is fantasy, an illusion, and that he is sitting at the keyboard. The only way for him to quit the game and come out of his stupor is to get through to the very end, or to die a lonely death in that virtual reality.

Sometimes, though, you encounter gamers (only a few), so-called divers, who do not ever lose their connection with reality; at any moment they can emerge fully from the Depths of the playing space—maybe to knock down a cold drink before a wild virtual adventure, or to launch some program which allows them to overcome more easily all the horrible dangers lying in wait for them in the Depths.

If I become one of these divers—that is, if I don't identify with the picture shown on the screen (in our model, with someone who plays according to the rules of the common world view), but rather with the person sitting at the key-board (the magician)—then, at just the right moment, I can quit the game (change the world around me).

What does mindfulness consist of? Remembering that *"I am a magician, and I, too, live in this illusory world, this projection of the common world view,"* and that *"I can change this world by connecting into the world of magic."* I do not believe that what happens in my life is inevitable; instead I respond to events by consciously choosing the most desirable outcome.

If necessary, I set my intention to creatively alter the situation. To manifest a chosen outcome, I enter into a magical state (*I can do anything!*)—eyes ablaze, heart sensuously warm, feeling like I'm on the verge of taking off into space…

This poem was written by a magician, who, in an attempt to increase her income, was hunting crocodiles while sitting naked on the edge of her bathtub, gently dipping her butt as bait into the water.

> Magic! Such a wondrous dream!
> Joyously it makes us free.
> May those who stipulate the rules
> Be bound themselves by their decree.
>
> From now on I'll strive to keep
> Only things which make me smile.
> Happily I'm dipping down
> My butt to lure a crocodile.

Since all world views are illusions, the magician laughs at the "rules of the game" and the "laws of the universe"—and at his own world view, too. He acts in *comedy theater* as opposed to the dramatic theater so adored by the rest of humanity. All the world is a theater of the absurd, pure hocus-pocus, distraction and mystification; why would you take any of it seriously? Instead, playful rituals like the crocodile hunt above are performed with joy, and miracles begin to happen...

This approach differs fundamentally from traditional conceptions, even from the theory of karma which is so fashionable these days. The beautiful karmic theater impresses by its drama. The idea of karma implies a heavy weight of sins and transgressions from the past. The only way to extirpate them is through repentance, penitence, and suffering, atoning for past mistakes over the course of a lifetime (or many lifetimes). Having ourselves once believed in the concept of karma, the question always rankled us: How can I possibly keep living with this impossibly heavy burden?! And what's more, it is we ourselves who have loaded this weight onto our own shoulders, having bought into the idea of karma, which, like any other world view, is really just another mass hallucination.

To be totally free while playing in the theater of cause and effect is extremely difficult—so much has already been absorbed into the personality. However, if you relate to karma in a light and easygoing way, with humor, then expiation of karma happens rather quickly and without suffering. You can absolve your karma over the course of your entire life (or over many lifetimes), or you can free yourself in a matter of months, days, hours, even minutes. Sometimes with a single, joyful wink, or skipping around playfully—and a thousand years of karma simply disappears without a trace.

GIVING THANKS

We don't take bribes, but we do accept tips.

Russian proverb

We have nothing to be afraid of except our fear.

Aphorism of a friend

There is no such thing as a problem without a gift for you in its hands. You seek problems because you need their gifts.

Richard Bach—*Illusions*

Once upon a time in a land far away, there lived a King and Queen. They had a daughter, Frosia, who was indescribably beautiful. The King had long considered how best to choose a worthy husband for the princess, when one night he had a dream, in which he saw his daughter imprisoned in a dark cave on a distant, unknown island named Buyan. This dream proved to be prophetic for soon thereafter the princess disappeared. Messengers were sent throughout the kingdom and ambassadors went overseas to proclaim the imperial decree: "Whoever finds the royal princess shall win her hand in marriage together with half the kingdom."

Princes and mighty warriors, merchants and common people responded to the call. The path to the island Buyan led through many dangerous trials and tribulations, requiring great deeds of strength, persistence, and courage. The trait most needed, however, was an unshakable belief in oneself. All these qualities were best shown by a peasant's son, Feodor.

While searching for the princess, Feodor became lost in a dense forest. Eventually, he came upon a faint trail which led him to a huge, moss-covered boulder. Through the moss and mold, Feodor could barely make out the inscription: "Go left and lose your head; go straight and find Koshchey;* go right and vanish into cyberspace!" Feodor sat down in deep thought. He didn't notice when an old woman, Dundusa, appeared before him out of nowhere.

"Why are you so sad, my friend? Why do you hang your head?"

"Don't disturb my thoughts, old woman. I'm miserable enough without you."

"You are not polite to your elders, Feodor."

"Get out of here, you old hag!"

"Take heed, Feodor, or you will regret this," the old woman warned, and she gradually melted into thin air.

It was late. Feodor was exhausted and fell into a heavy sleep. In his dream, Feodor was paddling down a turbulent river, the Kryamzha. Passing under a bridge, he caught a quick snatch of conversation: "It's such a terrible year for cranberries in the Vargun Bogs!"

The thought passed through his mind: "What do the Vargun Bogs have to do with me?"

Feodor felt hungry. He dragged his boat up a steep bank, lit a small fire, and cooked up a savory fish soup. Before eating, Feodor gulped down a slug of homebrew from his flask.

---

* In Russian folklore, Koshchey is an evil sorcerer of terrifying appearance, a shape-shifter, who often takes the form of a whirlwind. He is a nature spirit representing the destructive powers of nature. According to some sources, Koshchey might originally have been a kind wizard, whose image was gradually corrupted over time. [trans]

Suddenly, a sharp whistle startled him. Feodor peered across the river and gasped in astonishment. Dundusa was standing there, whistling at him and desperately waving her arms.

"What do you want, old woman?"

"Row me across the river, my dear."

"There's no time. I'm searching for my princess."

"Can't we just have a quick smoke together?"

"I don't smoke, old woman. I lead a healthy life."

Feodor continued on in his boat. For some time he pondered: "Why didn't I help that old woman? She was all alone there in the dark forest. Oh, to hell with her! She can take care of herself."

That night, while Feodor was sleeping soundly, someone stole his sword which bore the inscription: "For victory over the dragon Gorynych."

"There are thieves everywhere here! These borderlands are going to the dogs," he said indignantly. "Next time I'll camp further away from the village." But this did not comfort him at all.

The next day, still aggravated, Feodor became careless and did not notice a snag hidden amongst the weeds. At full speed, his boat crashed into the snag and flipped over. With difficulty he at last managed to reach the shore. So now all he had left was an old boat with a hole in it. Everything else had been swept away by the swift current. Feodor's teeth chattered violently; he just couldn't warm himself. His matches were all wet, and lighters were not yet invented. He began to feel feverish; his whole body was shaking. "When it rains, it pours!" Feodor managed to think as he was losing consciousness. "But there's nothing to be done. Life's tough for everyone these days."

When Feodor came to, the first thing he saw was Dundusa's familiar, wrinkled face.

"So, my dear friend, what mischief have you been up to?" she asked. "Now listen carefully to what I tell you:

"Once my nephew, the Mullah Nasrudin, couldn't make his donkey budge for anything, stopping him short on his journey to Mecca. Exhausted, he lay down to rest under a fig tree growing at the edge of a watermelon patch. Nasrudin looked at the watermelons, then at the fig tree and thought: 'Everything in this world is backwards. Those small vines bear huge melons, while this tall tree has only tiny figs.'

"The Mullah slipped into deep meditation, when suddenly a fig fell down from the tree, striking him on the head. This was so unexpected that he jumped up and, looking upwards, he saw a large monkey about to throw a whole handful of figs at him. The Mullah began thanking the monkey profusely.

"'*Thank you, monkey, for showing me that, if my every wish came true, then I wouldn't be able to thank you at all, since I would be buried beneath a whole pile of watermelons. How can I thank you enough?*'

"The monkey listened to this inspired discourse, still holding its handful of figs. Then the greatest magician of all time fished his prayer beads out of the folds of his robe and threw them up to the monkey. The monkey nimbly caught the beads and immediately hung them around its neck. The figs fell out of its hand, which caught the attention of the donkey, which ran over and started eating them. 'Eureka!' the Mullah exclaimed in a flash of realization.

"That's when he realized how to manage a stubborn donkey, and he immediately put his idea into practice. His donkey trotted happily after a bundle of hay hung on a stick in front of its nose, and the stick was attached to the body of the donkey."

Finishing her story, Dundusa began slowly evaporating into a rainbow cloud, which at last dissipated completely.

Feodor woke up and saw the same moss-covered boulder. He had hardly come back to his senses, when he heard a wild shout and crashing of branches. A furry ball rolled onto the footpath directly in front of him, scattering tufts of fur everywhere. Reaching Feodor, the ball split in half, and two demons stood before him. Cutting short their fight, they exclaimed gleefully: "Now we'll gobble you up, human!"

Feodor's hand, as usual, reached for his sword, but, seeing his movement, the demons burst into a wild frenzy of laughter. The older one took a toy cannon out of his pocket, which, in the twinkle of an eye, grew to full size.

"You still want to mess with us, little Feodor? You may have your humanity, but we have sorcery!" sneered the younger devil.

Feodor knew that he could not escape by running. He remembered his dream, and he could still hear Dundusa's voice uttering her parting words: *"Do not retreat and do not fight back, be nothing."* It dawned on Feodor that he should help the demons settle their conflict.

"Cease, cursed demons! Why are you fighting?"

"Our father died and we inherited a sack of gold, but we can't agree on how to divide it."

"That's not a problem. I can help you."

"If you cheat us, we'll eat you, but if you help us, we'll reward you well."

Feodor slyly winked at the older demon and suggested that he divide up the gold as evenly as possible. The older demon quickly split the gold into two piles. Then Feodor told the younger one to choose which pile he wanted. Both demons were happy with this solution.

"You are truly Solomon the Wise," rejoiced the demons, and they disappeared into the ground. At the very spot where they had vanished, a brand-new flying carpet appeared, still smelling of fresh dye. As Feodor took off flying up into the air, he noticed an inscription on the edge of the carpet: *"There is always a way out!"*

To understand how we deal with life's problems, we offer the following typical situation. Imagine that I'm walking down a dark street and notice the threatening figure of a street thug standing in my path. Fear rises inside me. In my imagination the pertinent movie automatically starts up, showing the thug coming up to me: "Gimme your wallet or I'll kill you!" I am already considering possible reactions—give him my money, knock him to the ground, turn and run. There are problems with each of these possible scenarios: I would hate to give up my hard-earned cash; I myself could end up being the one on the ground; and the thug (let's call him Ivan) might be a championship runner. What should I do? Or in the words of Hamlet: "To be, or not to be: that is the question: Whether 'tis nobler in the mind to suffer the slings and arrows of outrageous fortune [give him my money]. Or to take arms against a sea of troubles [carry mace]…"

For a magician, these questions make no sense whatsoever. Ivan indicates to the magician that it is time to get to work, to prove to himself that he is a magician.

Remember that at this point nothing has yet happened; the thug is still far away from me. Perhaps he hasn't even noticed me.

When a magician encounters a thug in a dark alleyway, he might say something like this (not necessarily out loud!):

"Thank you, Vanya,* for warning me that what I am imagining could actually happen to me: you could beat me up and take all my money. Then I might become like you, or end up begging for money at bus stops, since my wife would never let me come home without any money."

---

* *Vanya, Vanechka* (both stressed on the first syllabus)—endearing forms of the masculine name *Ivan*. [trans]

By speaking the thanksgiving monologue, we add a soundtrack to the "negative" internal movie which is showing in our mind. We can keep adding to it even to the point of absurdity, making it completely ridiculous. It is a well-known fact that expressing one's fear weakens it—the devil (fear) is not so terrible as he is painted (by people in their minds). The reason for this is that we pull fear out of the "subconscious" into the "conscious" mind, thus removing any "suppression."

The thanksgiving monologue is only the first part of the act of thanksgiving, but its recitation can instantly relieve the situation—for instance, someone might call out to the thug, distracting him, or a police car may pass by, or friends could emerge out of the next doorway; I might even exchange a few words with the thug and discover that we went to the same kindergarten, and so on.

It is important to note that, if fear did not rise in me when I first saw the thug, then I would not have to thank him.

I can "strengthen" the thanksgiving by sending Ivan *an imaginary gift*.

Imagine that someone picked out a gift for you, which was not only exactly what you wanted but was wrapped up in beautiful wrapping paper. We enjoy attractive packaging—a slender woman passing by, a shiny new Cadillac, a beautifully decorated cake, a well-dressed gentleman. There is a Russian proverb: "People meet your clothes, but accompany your mind."

While creating this imaginary picture, boundless scope for creativity opens up to the magician. He is not limited by the size of his canvas, range of colors, or rules prescribing his design. The artist prefers unusual images for these pictures, although there are also magicians who keep to a strict "classical" style. If we paint a tree, we might replace its fruit with doughnuts or soap bubbles, and the treetops could consist of colorful umbrellas. Russian fairytales are abundant in such images—Baba Yaga's hut on chicken legs, rivers of milk with jelly banks, the Frog Princess. In a more realistic style, we might paint the tree with a branchy top, a powerful root system, and thick, succulent leaves.

Now we can complete the act of thanksgiving for Ivan the thug:

"Thank you, Vanya, for warning me that what I am imagining could actually happen to me: you could beat me up and take all my money. Then I might become like you, or end up begging for money at bus stops, since my wife would never let me come home without any money. For warning me of this, I thank you and offer you a crane wearing rubber boots, which is painting a fence green with a vacuum cleaner."

During thanksgiving the gift may be transformed, and not only once. Beginning with a crane with a vacuum cleaner, we could leap to a monkey with a contrabass, which in turn could be transformed into a cave on the seashore, and so on. *Remember, the picture doesn't change by itself; it is you who draws and colors it in.*

You can close your eyes to help make your picture more vivid. If you are having difficulty creating the picture, just begin with any object which catches your eye. Suppose you see a button which you turn into a flying saucer, then a lake, a hockey puck, etc. After the initial image has been constructed, it is easy to adorn it with details.

In order to activate the imagination, we recommend that you bring sound to the process of drawing. Suppose that I am sitting in the kitchen, watching a running faucet. I say aloud: "I am drawing a waterfall in the mountains which hurls Feodor along in a barrel. He sits in it like Baba Yaga steering with a paddle, which he rented from a plaster statue at the Pioneer Camp 'Young Cavalryman.' On the bank below him, a Red Army soldier, Sukhov, greets him with traditional bread and salt. Sukhov is accompanied by freed women from the East, who are singing 'Like a snowflake, I melt in your arms...'"

We generally prefer to paint humorous pictures which are way over-the-top. When painting the crane, for instance, we place it in unusual circumstances. Every picture should have its own zest. A humorous frame of mind helps us create pictures easily, even playfully. Besides the visual channel, you can switch on the sound channel, and the sensory channel as well. As regards the crane, this could be the roar and vibration of the vacuum cleaner, the smell of paint, etc.

Let's look even deeper into the thanksgiving monologue. First, I thank the obstacle for warning me that my fear could be materialized. Remember, when the thug appeared, I immediately began playing in my imagination the horror movie called "How I Was Robbed" or "The Time I Got Beat Up." During the thanksgiving monologue, I add appropriate sound to the movie—more precisely, to its script—right up to its tragic finale. It is this tragic ending which really terrifies me.

Since magicians are such joyful people, the final scene in the thanksgiving monologue may even border on the grotesque. They intentionally lay it on so thick that it is impossible to stay serious, especially considering the reason for making this movie.

Consider how the obstacle strengthened in Feodor's dream as he paddled further down the Kryamzha River: the snatch of conversation heard about a bad cranberry harvest in a remote bog, his meal disrupted by Dundusa's whistle, the theft of his sword, crashing his boat, his illness. This is the thanksgiving monologue which Feodor should have recited immediately as he passed beneath the bridge:

"I thank you all for warning me that my journey is in peril. A poor harvest of potatoes and other crops may result in widespread

hunger. Gangs of bandits might appear in the forest, who will begin robbing tourists, and I could be stripped naked and hung by my feet from a tall pine tree..."

As a result of this thanksgiving, Feodor's dream would change, and this would influence daytime events. Feodor might receive a sign about what to do. It could be from a passing crow showing him the way he must travel, or the piercing shriek of an owl, or a leaf falling from a tree. But instead our hero had to sort things out with the demons.

If an act of thanksgiving is done with inspiration, in a single breath, you will not need to wait for results. Because of your creative state of mind, fear of the thug just disappears. However, if under the inertia of thinking fear returns, it is sufficient to remember the gift, or to make up a new one. If you get tired of the same, unchanging image of your gift, then you can further embellish the picture, enriching it with new detail—for instance, the crane might write a slogan on the green fence, which states: "Stand firm, little Mary!"

It is not by accident that we named the thug "Ivan." For convenience magicians have agreed to call all obstacles and problems by the generalized name—*Vanya*, or *dear Vanya*. This is especially handy when working with pain, fear, discomfort, and lack of self-confidence, when there is no specific object obstructing you (the thug in our example). However, a woman magician we know could not bear such discrimination against women and decided to name the obstacle Manya.*

By means of thanksgiving, the obstacle is transformed into success. The subject of such transfiguration is constantly encountered in Russian fairytales—Ivan the Fool, having passed through a thousand difficult trials, becomes Ivan the Prince.

---

* *Manya*—an endearing form of the feminine name *Maria*. [trans]

RESULTS OF MAGICAL ACTS

Of course, no one would say that Neznaika was hopelessly lazy. Once he learned to read properly, he would spend entire days with his books. He did not read books which were important, but rather books which were interesting, mainly fairytales… Neznaika often said that, if he had a magic wand, he could learn everything without trying; in fact, he would not need to learn anything at all, just wave his magic wand.

Nikolay Nosov —*Neznaika in Sun City*

When we plan neither for a definite result nor for sufficient time to attain it (not engaging the common world view), then the outcome often exceeds our wildest expectations.

Magicians have adopted a humorous unit of measurement—the "magical" number 27. To the question "When can I expect a positive outcome?" magicians answer: "In 27." They never specify what unit the reply is given in.

When I am soaring, all my intentions are realized. If an obstacle rises up to hinder me, I just remember that I am a magician and take creative action (e.g., express thankfulness). The world responds to my creativity, revealing the *best outcome for all participants* in this universal theater called life. I return to my state of soaring, and the situation resolves itself, often in a wholly unexpected way.

This is what happened to the magician Anna, who could not get along with a woman who worked under her. Finally, Anna decided to send her thanks—literally the next day, her subordinate found a better paying job and quit. They were both winners in this outcome.

A magician *does not plan the outcome, does not expect any particular result, and is prepared for anything—but hopes for the best.* This is the basic difference between the joyful magic presented in this book and wizardry, sorcery, and other systems which work for a particular result by imposing the will of the individual onto the outside world. You might say that the magician *invites* all the world to dance. Magicians are like the Russian fairytale character Emelia, who spends his day lounging around on the stove, while overseeing all the processes of the universe.

TECHNIQUES FOR RENAMING

"I come from under the hill, and under the hills and over the hills my paths led. And through the air. I am he that walks unseen."—"So I can well believe," said Smaug, "but that is hardly your usual name."—"I am the clue-finder, the web-cutter, the stinging fly. I was chosen for the lucky number."—"Lovely titles!" sneered the dragon. "But lucky numbers don't always come off."—"I am he that buries his friends alive and drowns them and draws them alive again from the water. I came from the end of a bag, but no bag went over me."—"These don't sound so creditable," scoffed Smaug."—"I am the friend of bears and the guest of eagles. I am Ringwinner and Luckwearer; and I am Barrel-rider," went on Bilbo beginning to be pleased with his riddling.

J.R.R. Tolkien—*The Hobbit*

"It is stupid for you to scorn the mysteries of the world simply because you know the doing of scorn," he said with a serious face.

I assured him that I was not scorning anything or any one, but that I was more nervous and incompetent than he thought.

"I've always been that way," I said. "And yet I want to change, but I don't know how. I am so inadequate."

"I already know that you think you are rotten," he said. "That's your *doing*. Now in order to affect that *doing* I am going to recommend that you learn another *doing*. From now on, and for a period of eight days, I want you to lie to yourself. Instead of telling yourself the truth, that you are ugly and rotten and inadequate, you will tell yourself that you are the complete opposite, knowing that you are lying and that you are absolutely beyond hope."

"But what would be the point of lying like that, don Juan?"

"It may hook you to another doing and then you may realize that both doings are lies, unreal, and that to hinge yourself to either one is a waste of time, because the only thing that is real is the being in you that is going to die. To arrive at that being is the not-doing of the self."

Carlos Castaneda—*Journey to Ixtlan*

The following legend is from a book by Deepak Chopra, *The Way of the Wizard*. One day Merlin pointed to King Arthur and offered a pouch of gold dust to anyone who could say who he truly was. There were various answers: the son of Uther Pendragon, the English Monarch, the flower of Albion, and so forth. In the end, Merlin cast the gold dust out the window, explaining that only the wind had given the correct answer—for the wind cannot speak.

Like King Arthur, each one of us has a number of roles and *masks* which we use while acting in the theater of life. In fact, the personality is this collection of masks. You can give a specific name to a particular mask, describing it in words, which is what King Arthur's courtiers did.

Since thought is material, we would state further that the environment around us corresponds to the particular mask which we wear. *When we change the mask, the circumstances around us likewise change*, as happened to the ugly duckling. As a chick it was relentlessly abused by the other birds, but when it finally matured into a beautiful swan, all birds sang its praises.

There is a well-known Zen Buddhist parable: Once a monk was being chased by a tiger. Running to escape, he reached the edge of a cliff. He climbed down a vine which hung over the edge only to see another tiger waiting at the bottom. At that point a mouse started nibbling at the vine. Caught in this predicament, the monk noticed a ripe strawberry growing off the face of the cliff. He stretched out his arm and tasted it. It was the most delicious berry he'd ever eaten! In the end the monk was saved; otherwise, he could never have told his story.

This brings us to the idea of *renaming* (switching the mask). The *diagnostic name* (old mask) of the monk sounds like this: "I am the one who is hanging by a vine being gnawed by a mouse, while tigers above and below lie in wait for me." But his new name is: *"I am the one who is eating a wild strawberry."*

Suppose an obstacle appears before me. I simply remember that I'm a magician and select a new mask. Consequently, my environment signals: "All OK!" And the obstacle disappears.

We need specific names to achieve our practical goals—*a formula for soaring (i.e., magical names)*. Here are some examples of these magical names: *"I am the one who serves my mother tea and raspberry preserves." "I am the one who elegantly pulls my pants up over my round belly." "I am Frekenbok who calls from the shower."*

In any magical act, the principal element is creativity—the free play of the imagination—so there is no requirement even to adhere to the formula "I am the one who…," or to think up any particular name. For example, participants at our seminars have achieved effective results using very unusual names like *"I am ordinary Soviet bamboo," "a Suck Hundred Mercedes," "a coat-hanger with yellow ears," "I am a lactating elephant with an evergreen trunk," "a sailor's splendid ass plying the great beer sea,"* or *"a real Indian is all right by me."*

Instead of renaming myself, I can instead rename the obstacle; after all, I am the one who created that obstacle (as well as everything else in my world view). For example, I often conflict with my mother-in-law. Her diagnostic name is: "I am the one who always makes a scene," but her new name has become: *"I am the one who tenderly pets the kitten."* In creating these names, it must be emphasized that my mother-in-law is in fact *me*. Instead of renaming my mother-in-law, I can rename my own being. *"I am the one who builds a shelf for my mother-in-law."* In the end, it does not really matter who is renamed; most important is to act creatively, and with good humor.

You may ask: "How long do I have to repeat a new name?" The amount of time is not determined by objective law—one person may require 27 seconds to resolve a complex problem, another 27 years, and a third 27 lifetimes. If I can laugh while watching myself "fettered" by some dramatic situation, then I will be freed fairly quickly.

To develop mindfulness, it is good to affirm my new name each time I notice myself falling back to my former name. If it is a long-standing name, then too many impressions are connected with it. For example, I have lived with my wife for ten years, and I have loved her for all these years. Suppose she suddenly leaves me for Ivan Ivanovich. Many different signals remain to remind me of her—a melody we would dance to, the park where we walked together, the smell of her perfume, her clothes, voice, our mutual friends... Instead of the old diagnostic name: "I am the one whose wife ran out on him," I must keep returning to my new name, and the situation manages in some way to resolve itself— my wife may come back, or I will meet the woman of my dreams, or perhaps women will cease to interest me...

Manifesting creativity, magicians not only repeat the new name, but also play it out in life. They dress up in silly costumes, utilizing attributes appropriate to the image they want to cultivate; they often compose verse, songs, or just some silly ditty. We will cover this in greater detail in the second part of this book, *Magical Stories*.

In this next section we will present specific renaming techniques.

RENAMING BY SEARCHING FOR THE ROOT

> Look to the root!
>
> Kozma Prutkov

Feodor rode his magic carpet for a long time, or was it a short time? He was intoxicated by his good fortune and did not notice a small speck which appeared in the clear, blue sky. Soon the speck grew into a small cloud. Finally seeing it, Feodor felt somewhat vexed, but at that point his attention was distracted by the witch Baba Yaga, laughing hysterically, as she zoomed past in her jet-propelled pestle.

"Nice engine, 27 dragon power. I wish I could have one of those!" thought Feodor, shivering from a sudden gust of wind. Raising his eyes, he saw the storm cloud now directly above him. A heavy shower suddenly drenched him. The carpet was soaked through and losing altitude rapidly. Feodor was only saved because, as he neared the ground, he managed to jump off at the last moment into an opportune haystack.

As he lay there recovering, the rain stopped, and a thick fog spread over the meadow. Feodor thought he could discern through the fog the familiar figure of Dundusa and prepared himself for yet another scolding. Dundusa spoke to him in her familiar nasal voice:

"When I was a young girl, my parents bought a summer cottage with a wonderful garden. In a corner of this garden, horseradish grew wildly with its huge leaves spreading out over

45

everything. Each week I would pull up the leaves, but they would always grow back again. Finally, I decided to *remove the entire root*. I dug a deep hole, but the root was thin, and it broke off. 'Stupid horseradish!' I thought, and left it at that. Through the rest of that summer, no more horseradish leaves appeared, and I forgot about them. Next spring I returned to the summer cottage and was shocked to find five thriving new horseradish plants where the one had grown before. I understood then the necessity of *digging down to the very end of the root!* Otherwise, the horseradish would eventually take over the entire garden. This time I dug down very carefully to where the root system ended, and removed it entirely. In its place I planted an apple tree, which even now produces unheard of bumper crops several times a year."

The fog cleared away, and Feodor thought: "What a bunch of nonsense! I must have hit my head when I fell."

However, Dundusa's reprimand had already entered into his subconscious, and he began to sort through various transportation mishaps which had occurred in his life. It was as if he was sinking deeper and deeper into his past.

Feodor recalled a vivid episode from his childhood. When he was three, his father had given him a scooter. Excited, Feodor rode it down to the road, where he met his neighbor, Grishka, who asked to try it out. Feodor refused and moved on. Then, like a devil out of a snuff box, the hobgoblin Kuzia jumped out onto the roadway and snatched away his scooter. Feodor ran home crying his eyes out and, to make matters worse, his father gave him the belt for what had happened.

"It's too bad I didn't let Grishka have a ride," concluded Feodor. He imagined himself giving the scooter to Grishka, who suggested that they go down to the river to try it out on the steep hill there. Feodor experienced an indescribable *sense of freedom* and speed as he raced down the hill.

Suddenly Feodor heard a strange noise. A Russian stove rose up from behind a nearby haystack. Laying on the stove was an odd-looking fellow in a fur cap.

"Do you want a lift?" he asked.

"Sure, thanks."

"Lie down here. It'll be more fun traveling together."

The stove drifted off out of sight to the sound of balalaikas and heroic singing.

Here is a real-life story of a magician named Varya:

I returned home on the 23rd of February.* My son was drinking wine with his friends. This disturbed me very much, so I began searching my past for an episode when I had been frightened by a drunken man for the very first time. I recalled an incident when I was three years old, in a flash remembering it in great detail. We were waiting at home for our father. My sister was doing her homework, my grandmother was cooking. Father just wouldn't come home! My grandmother told us that he would probably show up drunk, and she advised us: "You are always hanging all over your daddy, but instead you should say to him: 'Shame on you!' Maybe then he will stop his drinking. The neighbor boy told his father that, and he hasn't been drunk for two weeks!"

Our father finally arrived home and we said exactly what grandmother had told us to say. An argument broke out. Father raised his hand against mother, and she ran away. Then he threw an overcoat at Grandmother to shut her up. My sister said something mean to him and also ran away. I was left all alone, sitting on a chair. Even though I loved

* Red Army Day—in Russia this day is celebrated like Father's Day. [trans]

my father very much, I told him that he was a drunken pig. He rushed at me, threatening to strike me with his hand.

I replayed this scene in my mind but altered it. In the new version, I persuaded Grandmother to bake pies to welcome father when he came home. I began repeating my new name: *"I am the one who welcomes father with pies."* Over time my son stopped carousing with his drinking buddies, and eventually enrolled in college, where he found new friends.

We can analyze this story in the following way. The diagnostic name of Varya is: "I am the one who is troubled by my son's drinking." In order to deal with his drinking problem, she utilizes the technique of *searching for the root*. Varya must recall the first episode in her life when a drunken person disturbed her peace of mind, and then to select a new name to reprogram the root episode. If she is having difficulty finding the root, she can trace back the chain of similar experiences in her life, beginning with the most recent. Gradually, untying knot after knot, she will finally arrive at the first such experience in her life—the root episode. Varya was able to reach that root episode—her father's arrival home drunk when she was three. At that point, she had two methods to choose from.

First method: Varya must *search for an act of thankfulness* associated with the obstacle (her father), which happened at around the same time as the root episode. For example, Varya recalled that once on her father's birthday she had drawn a picture for him which depicted her mother, grandmother, and friends giving him flowers, balloons, and other gifts. Her father was very touched and still today has this picture. This act of thankfulness is incorporated into her formula for soaring: *"I am the one who draws a picture of daddy's birthday."*

Second Method: Varya goes back in her memory to the very threshold of the root episode, when everything was still unclouded, when nothing yet foretold the coming drama. Then she will be able *to reenact the events according to a new script*, sending her father inner peace. The new script states that Varya persuaded her grandmother to bake pies to welcome her father, and this was incorporated into her new name.

This second method of renaming is often utilized by the heroes of the film *Back to the Future*. Varya preferred this method, although both can be equally valuable, depending on the situation. Feodor also used this method when he gave his scooter to Grishka. If it is difficult for you to remember an appropriate act of thankfulness, then apply the *"Back to the Future"* method.

People have a strong belief in the law of cause-and-effect. For this reason, the technique of renaming by searching for the root (the cause) is extremely effective. It is often used in psychotherapy, but apparently is a very ancient method. In the works of Carlos Castaneda, he describes one of the main techniques of don Juan—re-examination, based on researching one's past.

Serge Kahili King, in his book *Urban Shaman*, gives many examples of this technique. He tells an amazing story about a woman in California who severely burnt her leg on the exhaust pipe of a motorcycle. For a long time the burn would not heal, so she started picturing in her mind a different, better scenario in which she did not touch the exhaust pipe, weaving it around in her imagination forty times. The results were very impressive—the severe wound skinned over in only three days. Many of the ideas and techniques in this outstanding book have much in common with our own world view.

In neuro-linguistic programming (NLP), a similar technique is widely utilized called "changing one's personal history." Recently in Russia the idea of karma, thanks largely to the works of Sergey Nikolaevich Lazarev, has begun to penetrate into the mass consciousness. The technique of renaming by searching for the root, which, in fact, alters karma, is gradually becoming better understood and accepted. Also, various methods for renaming by searching for the root are fundamental to Holodynamics and Dianetics.

The effective use of this technique of searching for the root is based on the fact that, as a rule, a person can recall vivid scenes from his own life while plunging deeply into childhood memories. We experience once again those intense emotions which only a child can feel.

Following are some guidelines for those who wish to use this technique of renaming to work with clients.* First, the person must clearly state the issue at hand. Next, the client seeks out an earlier episode in life which is similar to the current issue and, continuing to trace the chain of similar experiences back in memory, finally discovers the root episode. This root episode is considered the primary cause of the issue which is currently manifesting in the client's life. Generally, root episodes occur in early childhood. In order to help a person *remember the root*, you can try narrating stories showing how others have *recalled* root episodes. Sometimes, following established practice, you can narrate several stories, inserting one into the other (the so-called spiral of Milton Erickson). An example of working in this way is described in the story narrated in the second section called "This is no way to treat a pregnant woman!"

The question is often asked: What should I do if I can't remember the root episode? There are various options: stubbornly keep trying until you finally discover the unfortunate event; remember a similar episode and proclaim it the root; or switch to a different technique.

* The techniques described in this book can be used for resolving the issues of others. Many examples of working with clients are contained in the magical stories given in the second section.

RENAMING THE ACTUAL OBSTACLE

"Every single thing's crooked," Alice thought to herself, "and she's all over pins!"

"May I put your shawl straight for you?" she added
aloud, "…and dear me, what a state your hair is in!"

Alice carefully released the brush, and did her best to
get the hair into order.

Lewis Carroll—*Alice through the Looking Glass*

Feodor and Emelia rode along on top of the stove.

"How can I possibly find my princess?" Feodor asked.

"What the hell do you need her for?"

"I'm in love with Frosia. The world is nothing to me without her," he replied.

Seeing that Feodor was imprisoned by yet another illusion,
the wise magician understood that it was too early to accept
him as his apprentice.

"At least I can teach him to work with the actual obstacle,"
thought Emelia.

"Take this path, Feodor. It will lead you to a palace which
is not a palace, and a cottage which is not a cottage. There you
will find that which no one knows. If you can manage to take
that with you, it will help you find your princess.

Feodor embraced Emelia, climbed down from the stove,
and set off down the path. It led him to a small cottage with
no windows or porch. He entered stealthily and hid behind

the stove. Suddenly, a dwarf with a long beard walked into the cottage and shouted:

"My friend, Khron! I'm hungry!"

Out of nowhere a table appeared laden with a barrel of beer and a roasted bull with a sharp knife stuck in its side. The dwarf sat down at the table, pulled out the knife, and began slicing the meat, dipping each piece in garlic before eating it; he was thoroughly enjoying his meal. He finished off the roast to the last bone while drinking down the entire barrel of beer.

He commanded: "My friend, Khron! Clear the table!" The table instantly disappeared as if it had never existed.

Feodor stayed in hiding until the dwarf left. Stepping out from behind the stove, he gathered up his courage and called out:

"My friend, Khron! Feed me!"

Out of nowhere a table appeared laden with various dishes, appetizers, desserts, and various wines and meads. Feodor sat at the table and said:

"My friend, Khron! Come sit down with me! Let's eat and drink together."

An invisible voice replied:

"Thank you, my good man. How many years have I served here and yet have never been offered so much as a burnt crust, but you have invited me to share your meal."

Feodor looked around and wondered: "No one is visible, and yet food is vanishing piece by piece from the table. The wines and meads are pouring themselves; the goblet gallops around all by itself."

"My friend, Khron! Show yourself to me!"

"That's impossible; no one can see me. I am that which no one knows."

"My friend, Khron! Would you like to be my servant?"

"Why not? I see that you're a kind person."

And they went away together.

The technique of searching for the root, as elucidated in the previous section, compels us to delve deeply into our past. It is sometimes easier, though, to apply instead a technique we call *renaming the actual obstacle*. This technique is illustrated in the following story told by Andrey. It depicts a typical example of working with the actual obstacle.

One night I was driving my family home and inadvertently ran a stoplight. It was very late, when there are no cars and, more important, no traffic cops. So I was completely surprised when an officer with a striped baton appeared out of nowhere. He signaled for me to stop. He looked frozen stiff, standing there alone in his thin boots. There was a heavy frost outside, and the officer was unconsciously tapping out a dance with his feet, which were obviously freezing! In my mind I offered him a glass of vodka, then hot tea with honey, and, to top it off, heavy boots trimmed with reindeer fur. At that very moment, the officer—royal knight of urban crosswalks—relaxed his forehead, and the stern furrows crossing his brow smoothed over. I started repeating to myself: *"I am the one who gives boots to the royal knight of urban crosswalks."* He let me off with hardly a slap on the wrist.

In this technique you first study the obstacle, and then mentally offer various acts which "improve"* that obstacle. If the obstacle is immediately "improved" as a result of your mental gift, then you have found the correct renaming formula. If the obstacle is not "improved," or has even "worsened" (not likely), you then just pretend that it actually was "improved" and compose a formula for soaring.

---

* Quotation marks signify that the improvements which I strive for are *based on the assumptions of my personal world view.*

Renaming by Finding the Ray of Light

When you look into the ashes, look well.

Deepak Chopra—*The Way of the Wizard*

If you find yourself in darkness, and all you see is one pale ray of light, you must walk straight toward it, without speculating whether or not there is any sense in it. Perhaps there really is no sense in it, but certainly there is no sense to just sit in the darkness.

Victor Pelevin—*Hermit and Six-Toes*

Feodor turned to his invisible companion:

"Please help me find my princess, my friend Khron."

"There is a certain very old frog, who knows where to find her. She has lived in the bogs for three hundred years. Go seek her out, but without me, as there is nothing there for me. I have an aunt who lives in a kingdom far, far away. She is a sensitive woman, and just today she sent me a telepathic message, asking me to visit her. Release me, Feodor, but if you should need me, call out my name, and I will find you."

"Go, my friend Khron."

Feodor set off for the Lower Vargun Bog. This was much easier said than done. He wandered around lost for a long time, or was it a short time? Finally he reached the bog and called out:

"Grandmother Frog! Are you alive?"

"I am alive."

"Please come out to me from the bog."

The old frog slowly crawled out of the bog.

"Do you know where I can find the Princess Frosia?"

"Once I could show you the way, but now I'm so old. I can no longer leap very far, and a River of Fire blocks the way. No animal can leap over it, nor bird fly over it. Only I could cross it, when I was a young COMSOMOL* member, but now I can't."

"Tell me more about yourself. You must have seen much in your long life."

"I have been starving for many years, and all my strength is lost. But there once was a time when I'd bathe myself in warm milk which would rejuvenate me, and then I could jump all the way to the edge of the world. But where can I get milk now? Hopping to the village would be the death of me."

Feodor went to the village, found a cow, and brought back a pail of milk. He set Grandmother Frog in it and brought her to the River of Fire. At its edge, Feodor took Grandmother Frog out of the pail and set her on the ground.

"Now, dear friend, sit down on my back," she commanded

"What are you saying, Grandmother? You're so small. I'll squash you!"

"Don't worry, you won't squash me. Just sit down and hold on tight."

Feodor mounted Grandmother Frog and she began to swell up. She grew bigger and bigger until she was as large as a haystack.

"Are you holding on tight?"

* COMSOMOL is the Young Communist League, a mass youth group during the Soviet Era. [trans]

"Yes, Grandmother."

She continued to swell up bigger and bigger until she was larger than the dark forest. And then how she leaped! She sailed high over the River of Fire.

"Now, Feodor, we are on the island Buyan. From here the princess is only a stone's throw away."

We will now examine yet another world view, which correlates with the principle of duality popular in the East known as "Yin and Yang." Within any object you can find a creative element, and within every destructive phenomenon there exists a spark of life—the *ray of light*. For example, a tree which is withering yet still has powerful roots, or a mangy dog which still leads the pack.

The technique of renaming by finding the ray of light is simple: I locate this ray, the source of strength, and it leads me to success. In our examples, you might compose names like these: *"I am the one who grows powerful roots,"* and *"I am the one who leads the pack."* The following story told by a magician illustrates how this translates into real life.

I was on the subway. Sitting at the back of the car were two filthy homeless guys in torn coats carrying wooden walking sticks. But each held in his hands a very thick book which they were fully engrossed in. At the next stop, another homeless fellow entered and moved through the car begging for money. He looked terrible. Not only was he dirty, but he was also injured. He had a black eye, and there were several cuts on his bloodied shaven head. He stopped in front of me and, without thinking twice, I gave him some money.

The two other vagrants began discussing loudly how life was no easier for them, but nobody ever gave them money, and they would never fall so low as to beg. I realized that I had taken their bait, they had aroused my pity. There were very few people on the car, but their ruckus was irritating everyone, and some people told them to settle down. Instantly I saw the ray of light—they were homeless but were reading, and what thick books! In my mind I spoke the name: *"I am the one who is reading a very thick book."* The car became quiet. The injured fellow stopped begging for money and squatted down by the doors, and the two others opened their books to continue reading.

Imaginative renaming

Alice looked all round her at the flowers and the blades of grass, but she could not see anything that looked like the right thing to eat or drink under the circumstances. There was a large mushroom growing near her, about the same height as herself; and, when she had looked under it, and on both sides of it, and behind it, it occurred to her that she might as well look and see what was on top of it. She stretched herself up on tiptoe, and peeped over the edge of the mushroom, and her eyes immediately met those of a large blue caterpillar that was sitting on the top, with its arms folded, quietly smoking a long hookah, and taking not the smallest notice of her or of anything else.

Lewis Carroll—*Alice's Adventures in Wonderland*

If you have imagination as a grain of sesame seed... all things are possible to you.

Richard Bach—*Illusions*

Meanwhile, the princess was languishing in captivity, and dark thoughts crowded her mind:

"What if no one rescues me? Will the best years of my life be wasted in this hole?"

Water dripped monotonously from the ceiling of the cave and, hypnotized by the sound, the princess fell into a deep sleep.

She dreamed that she was found by a terrifying, hunch-backed beast with crooked arms, claws, and hooves. He had a hooked nose, long fangs protruding from his mouth, and was completely covered in hair. Frosia started shouting hysterically and frantically waved her small, white hands in the air.

"Now I'll have to endure a long life of suffering married to this horrible beast! I'd rather throw myself under a speeding train than live with that thing!"

The princess lay there grief-stricken for some time, but there was nothing else to do—the wedding was set for the following day. She decided to try to improve her attitude: "Could there possibly be anything about him I could ever love?"

She took a closer look at the beast and noticed that he had kind eyes. They were shining with an inner smile, and those eyes began to hypnotize Frosia. The beast transformed first into a shining cocoon, then into a New Russian. He was dressed in a crimson-colored tuxedo with gold buttons, lots of gold chains and rings, and a fashionable, spiky haircut. With a victorious shout "Bonsai!" she threw her arms around the neck of the former beast, and kissed him passionately with her sugary lips. Then the second transfiguration happened. The new Russian turned into a hero more handsome than could be described in any fairytale, or by any pen. The princess woke up and the handsome hero of her dream was standing there by her side. Of course, it was Feodor.

Let's say an obstacle rises up before me—my wife is furious and threatening me with an iron skillet. I immediately compose an internal movie—for instance, a Centaur selling sunflower seeds at the marketplace. Then I choose a name: *"I am a Centaur who sells roasted sunflower seeds."*

Magicians prefer to imagine new, even extraordinary movies, which usually do not have analogues in the common world view—a Centaur as a sunflower seed vendor.

I *consciously create* this movie myself, not waiting for an image to just appear. Usually this happens very quickly, although sometimes it seems that the internal pictures exist in and of themselves, that I "see" them.

Many magicians have their own personal method for creating imaginary pictures. Some shut their eyes, so as not to be disturbed by their surroundings. Sparks, dots, stripes, and patches of color float through their internal sight, coalescing into familiar images—people, wild animals, cars… One of our friends prefers to think up images while looking at objects sideways. don Juan suggests defocusing the glance (c.f. the works of Carlos Castaneda).

Following are two examples of imaginative renaming:

Every evening for many years I could clearly hear through my walls my elderly neighbors drinking heavily with their friends. They would get completely smashed! I dreaded each evening and had trouble falling asleep. My repeated complaints to the police brought no results.

One day I went to a seminar on magic and became acquainted with the technique of imaginative renaming, which I decided to apply to my problem. Starting with the drunken voices resounding in my head, I imagined a thick Chinese crayon. One half of the crayon was blue, and the other half red. In my mind I sharpened the red half of the crayon and heard the name: *"I am the one who is sharpening the red end of the crayon."* To my utter amazement, the drunken revelry ended that very night. My neighbors had simply stopped drinking.

One evening my husband Pavel dragged into the house a whole slew of electronic components and tried to put them together into a computer. After some time, he burst into the room, yelling: "Don't even come near me! Nothing's working out!"

Usually I would be completely crushed by his comments, but this time I imagined that *I was basking on the hot sand* on a sun-drenched desert island.

I felt relief from this picture but still harbored doubts deep in my heart: "What if nothing works out for Pavel, and that horrible scene happens again?" I went into the kitchen, poured a whole pile of semolina onto a plate, and put it in the microwave. After several minutes, I pulled out the plate and stuck my hands into the warm "sand."

My son came in, asking: "What're you doing?"

I answered: "Warming my hands."

He came up and started playing with the semolina and, inspired and invigorated, I decided to iron the linen. My mood was remarkably good, and I completely forgot that my husband was angry. Pavel again entered the room. He had calmed down somewhat and, stating that it still wasn't working out, he immediately withdrew. I remembered *basking on the hot sand*. As I continued ironing, Pavel stepped once more into the room and, with complete calm, stated: "You know, nothing is going right today. Let's have some tea together."

Pavel didn't work on the computer any more that day, but his mood was fine. The next day Pavel bought some more components, and the computer started working.

Support signals

It became completely quiet all around. The flowers
sprung up. And the Divine Gnome fluttered from flower to
flower, collecting sweet nectar in a green, enameled mug.
"We drink to our victory in grievous battle!" he proclaimed cheerfully and in a single gulp drained the mug.
                    Evgeny Kliuev—*Between Two Chairs*

If I watch for *support signals*—auspicious events which occur
around me—this signifies that I am in harmony. Whatever I do
will turn out well, I see success and happiness everywhere I turn.
The following narrative shows a chain of support signals.

I had just walked up to the traffic signal *as the green
light came on.* I crossed the street, and right away *a half-
empty bus rolled up,* which took me to the subway station.
I descended to the platform, and directly in front of me
the train doors flew open. In the subway car, I immediately
found an empty seat, and *an elegant woman with a bouquet
of spectacular roses* sat down opposite me. At the subway
exit, a young man, *smiling broadly,* stepped forward *with
arms outspread to greet the woman.* On the street, I saw *a
man whirling around in a rousing dance* to the pleasure of
a crowd of spectators. From the loudspeaker, which hung
on the building wall a few yards from the dancer, a song
blared out: *"You shall have all that you desire…"*

It was obvious that everything would turn out well for me that day.

Because I was in a state of soaring, *my plans and projects were realized*, my wishes were fulfilled. Consciousness of oneself as a magician creates the conditions required so that all life's needs happen of themselves. Only time is required to draw success to me. And if it doesn't come immediately, I won't fall into despair.

There is a well-known Indian parable:

Once Shiva came down to earth. There he saw a holy Brahman, who for his entire life had endured the harshest asceticism and observed all the rituals, constantly praying to Shiva. The Brahman asked the Three-Eyed One:

"Oh, Mahadeva, when will I attain enlightenment?"

"You have only one incarnation left."

At these words, the Brahman became furious and started cursing Shiva, insisting that he had already earned enlightenment in this life. With these words, the Brahman no doubt extended his term of confinement in human form for many more lifetimes.

Next Shiva passed by a tipsy peasant who was making love to another man's wife. The peasant asked the Six-Armed One:

"Oh, Mahadeva, when will I attain enlightenment?"

"You still have ten incarnations to go."

The peasant, wild with joy, broke into a dance, singing ecstatically: "And in the end I will be free!"

At that moment he attained enlightenment.

RENAMING ON THE WING

I'm the lantern that keeps burning dimly at night,
I'm the cricket that sits on the furnace so bright,
I'm the blind whose smooth breast hides the light of the moon,
I'm the snoring that drives silence out of the room.

I'm the pen which allows you to write lines in stride,
I'm the note or the letter which lies to one side,
I'm the hosepipe with languid bliss coated,
I'm the rustle of leaves barely noted.*

Following is a story by a certain magician we know:

I was preparing for a job interview. It had been overcast
all day, but when I left my house, the sun was just peeping
out. On the subway, my attention was drawn to a fancily
dressed woman. *An inscrutable smile floated across her face,
and something fluffy—like a fox's tail but canary-colored—circled around her neck. Knitted gloves dangled from the sleeves
of her lavender jacket.* Emerging onto the street, I admired
the *bright, blue sky with a few wispy clouds rose-tinted by the
setting sun.* Based on these support signals, I concluded
that the interview would go well, and that the work would
prove to be a perfect fit for me. And so it turned out.

* This poem was translated by John Woodsworth. [trans]

An unbroken chain of support signals rising before me confirms that I am in a state of soaring. If not, I can enter the state by using the simple technique of *renaming on the wing*. I begin by *continuously* composing new formulas for soaring by noticing the pleasing and amusing scenes around me. I find something good in everything occuring within my field of vision.

For example, in the story just cited, I could compose a sequence of names: *"I am the sun peeping out," "I smile inscrutably," "I am a fluffy, canary-colored tail circling around a neck," "I am knitted gloves dangling from the sleeves of a lavender jacket," "I am the one who rose-tints the wispy clouds high up in the blue sky."* While renaming on the wing, I quickly enter into a state of soaring. If at the same time I also *embody* that name into my entire being—that is, I portray physically the sun peeping out, the furry tail circling a neck, etc.—then the result can be stunning. The following story illustrates the technique of renaming on the wing.

My friend Valeria, who trusts my taste, asked me to help her choose a nightstand to match her furniture. So one morning, she and her husband picked me up in their car. We drove all over Samara, but we could not find an acceptable piece anywhere.

I began renaming on the wing. I immediately noticed a sign advertising: "You know, everything will happen in time!" I composed the name: *"I am that which you know will happen in time!"* I saw a sign for the Department of Motor Vehicles: "Every child on the road is your own!" I became *"someone else's child who's never on the road."* Next, I saw a woman in a fur coat carrying a pink makeup bag. A tiny kitten was scampering after her . It looked comical, and I said to myself: *"I am a pink makeup bag in a fur coat walking a kitten."* I saw a dog curled up asleep in a cardboard box: *"I am the one who is sleeping in a cardboard box.* " I experienced an inexpressible happiness from all this, noticing only the positive signals, which were striking in their uniqueness. It was as if I were a relay wand being passed from one signal to the next.

When we drove by one particular store, I felt like going in and asked my friends to stop the car. Right at the entryway, I caught sight of the curtains of my dreams, and at a very low price. I had long been planning to redecorate my bedroom with new curtains, but I only had three hundred rubles on me; they cost a thousand. Unable to let go, I thought: "Wait a minute, I'm a magician!" I noticed a delicate tassel dangling down from "my" curtains, so I renamed myself as *"a tassel adorning the curtains."*

I'm not sure why I went up to the second floor, where automobile parts were sold. There I met my dear friend Vasya, whom I had not seen for three years. We hugged each other warmly, and he said: "Please forgive me. I called you several times to repay you the money I borrowed, but I just couldn't ever get ahold of you."

"What do you mean? What money?"

"Don't you remember? We were going to Natasha's birthday party, and you lent me money to buy her a present."

I finally did recall the present we bought her, and also that I paid Vasya's share. Vasya quickly converted the debt into dollars at the rate of three years ago, multiplied it by today's rate, and announced an astronomical sum which he promised to pay back immediately.

"I'd rather borrow it from you for now; I don't have enough cash on me for the curtains."

"C'mon, let's go. I'll buy them for you."

Altogether Vasya gave me seven hundred rubles, and I left the store with the package under my arm. Valeria was staggered. I was exhilarated, though, and continued renaming on the wing. Suddenly, right in front of me was an astounding sight: an old man smiling from ear to ear, his gray beard fluttering in the wind, wearing a black cap and a priest's robe with a blue jacket over it, and skis (!) under his arm. "Could I be dreaming?" I asked myself. Valeria was talking to her husband, so they didn't even notice this amazing spectacle.

At the time we were passing by a department store, and I noticed an advertisement on the corner: "Furniture for sale, enter next right." For no apparent reason, I blurted out: "That store has the perfect nightstand for you!"

As we were parking, I thought: "What if I'm wrong? What will I say if they don't have any?"

Entering the store, we immediately saw two inlaid nightstands in oak veneer. They were still being sold at old prices, so instead of the seven thousand rubles my friends expected to pay, they cost only three. You can only imagine the astonished looks they gave me.

Let's turn our attention to the name: *"I am that which you know will happen in time!"* Such a name is constructed on the basis of an ingenious principle used by ancient bards: "I sing what I see."

The idea of renaming on the wing is wonderfully expressed in the poetry of the magician Petr Dmitryev:

> I am the cold and wintry day,
> To north winds I give no resistance.
> I am the stout old stump and stay
> There sticking out with firm persistence.
>
> For lovers I am the secluded
> Corner in the garden haven.

I am the huge (with leaves protruding)
Maple with its helpful raven.

I am that raven's excrement,
And hurl myself with inspiration
On a flight of welcoming intent—
A hat serves as my landing station.

I hide a languid gaze as a narrow
And foxy eyelash—yes, that's me,
I love to chase the wayward sparrow:
I'm just a happy chickadee.

I am a big old garbage-can
I am the useless trash within it.
A chicken-rib is what I am—
A mangy cat comes gnawing on it.

I am its purring, still, sublime,
On knees so huge they're simply frightful.
I am a flask of Georgian wine,
To drink me is a taste delightful.

I am the moon with stately head
So bright amidst the sky all darkening.
I am the cockroach on white bread,
The ravenous plague, to all disheartening.

I am the paving stone dejected,
On which fine steeds may trot clip-clop.
I am the glove, perfume-infected,
Which ladies sometimes will let drop.

I am the bright green traffic light
On a road with dusty incrustations,
A motor-car revving with all its might
As I speed to hidden destinations.*

Following is the author's experience of the day's events reflecting this poem:

Waking up, I open the curtains and look outside. The day is cold and windy. My glance falls on a dog running around a huge tree stump. On level with the window, a raven sits perched on a branch. Below it, a girl in an old-fashioned bonnet walks past... I catch sight of a chickadee stealing breadcrumbs from a sparrow.

I gather my things and head downstairs to the entryway, scaring off a couple of lovebirds hiding in a secluded nook. Right then, a spry old woman overtakes me carrying her trash can (in our building there are no garbage chutes). Walking out onto the street, I notice a mangy old cat gnawing a chicken bone. I imagine the cat purring on the old woman's lap as she gently strokes its fur.

There is an empty wine bottle next to the trash bin and a stale crust of bread. I imagine the joy a cockroach must feel when it happens upon such a hefty slice of bread—a hearty meal! I recall eating such a piece of bread yesterday evening, sitting in the kitchen admiring the moon.

I warm up the car and drive off. Alongside the road, a huge billboard depicting a horse attracts my attention. This brings to mind a horse's hooves clattering over the cobblestones. Later on, I catch sight of a glove fallen onto the pavement. Straight ahead a green traffic light emerges out of the gloom...

* This poem was translated by John Woodsworth. [trans]

TESTING THE WATERS

"What you saw was not an agreement from the world," he said. "Crows flying or cawing are never an agreement. That was an omen!"

"An omen of what?"

"A very important indication about you," he replied cryptically.

At that very instant the wind blew the dry branch of a bush right to our feet.

"That was an agreement!" he exclaimed and looked at me with shiny eyes and broke into a belly laugh...

"This is very weird," I said, "but I feel really good."

I heard the cawing of a crow in the distance. He lifted his finger to his right ear and smiled.

"That was an omen," he said.

A small rock tumbled downhill and made a crashing sound when it landed in the chaparral. He laughed out loud and pointed his finger in the direction of the sound.

"And that was an agreement," he said.

Carlos Castaneda—*Journey to Ixtlan*

When I set a goal, a corresponding internal movie is launched. I then witness the process of achieving that goal in the outer world, often in a modified form. By observing the events (the *signs*) unfolding around me, I can determine what kind of effort, and how much, will be required to secure the desired result.

An unfavorable sign, in the form of an obstacle, portends potential difficulties in achieving the goal. The easier it is to remove an obstacle, the less time and effort will be necessary.

Suppose someone calls me to propose that I buy a large shipment of flour at a favorable price. While I'm talking, *my coffee boils over.* After the phone call, as I'm cleaning the stove, I tip over the coffeepot spilling the leftover coffee, which settles into *an aromatic puddle* in the middle of the kitchen floor. Frustrated and angry, I suddenly "see the light"—I realize the source of the trouble, and decide to turn down the deal to purchase the flour. In the end, another friend purchases it and suffers a huge loss.

Another example: I am invited to a business meeting. Before leaving my house, I hear on the television the following commercial:

"Today is a *critical day* for me, so I can't go roller skating with you."

"You should try *Always* sanitary pads."

"Now that I use Always *sanitary pads, I can go roller skating any day I want, not that I'm all that good a skater."*

I understand from the commercial that this is a critical day for me; it would be pointless for me to go to the meeting. But the ad also communicates that, if I go to the meeting carrying these magical sanitary pads, then success will be assured. What's more, I can go at any time. The end of the commercial tells me that there is still much for me to learn. So I buy a pack of sanitary pads and take them with me to the meeting, which turns out very successfully.

If I observe the support signals—"agreements from the world," as don Juan puts it—it means that my plan is patterned after that of all creation. However modest, it becomes part of the greater plan of Nature. Once I was planning a business trip to Samara and went to buy my ticket. At the cashier's window, there was one person ahead of me, who bought a ticket... to Samara! The business trip exceeded all my expectations.

When faced with a difficult choice, I first *test the waters*. Suppose I can't decide whether to sell an apartment now or to wait. Noticing a raven perched on a tree outside my window, I assign it the role of arbiter: if in the next 27 seconds the raven defecates, then I should sell the apartment immediately; if it takes longer, then I'd better wait; if the raven flies away or doesn't show any inclination to defecate, then I shouldn't sell the apartment at all. I have hardly established these conditions in my mind, when the raven poops. I know then that I can start selling the apartment right away without worrying, knowing that the transaction will proceed quickly and profitably.

People throughout the ages have always tested the waters using various means. This process is really just another form of divination—like reading animal entrails, clouds, cards, runes, coins, daisies, etc. Magicians approach divination creatively, devising extraordinary methods for testing the waters.

I had to go to the pharmacy to buy some medicine. They were out at the store near my home, so I walked to the bus stop thinking: "If a bus comes, I will walk in that direction, but if a trolley comes, then that other direction." At that moment, an express bus raced past me, so I followed it in a third direction. Soon I found a pharmacy, which had the medicine at the old prices—in fact, at half-price!

The result of testing the waters does not necessarily give a final verdict. When something attracts me, but signs warn me of difficulties, I can face these difficulties directly and play the renaming game. As the saying goes: "Desire makes the impossible—possible." In any good short story, film, or play, the hero always overcomes a series of obstacles, which forms the basic plot of the work. This often gives people the impression that the purpose of life consists of constantly surmounting hurtles and passing through various hardships. We do not share this point of view—we enjoy living with ease, not tangling ourselves up in plans which only create problems for ourselves and others.

Note:

The authors do not accept claims like this:

"I tested the waters as described in your book but in the end had to 'muddle through a puddle.' I challenge you to a duel!"

By this very assertion, the plaintiff has renounced his power as a magician, attempting to shift the responsibility for his behavior onto Uncle Vasya. The art of testing the waters, like all the techniques given in this book, requires practice.

CONCLUSION TO THE THEORETICAL SECTION

Everything in this book may be wrong.

Richard Bach—*Illusions*

The magician's techniques described in this book are just some of many possibilities for helping people unlock their creativity. Magic is not a dogma; it is a course of action. Express your creativity! *Develop your own techniques and personal world view!* The techniques are not the point. You simply must know that you are a magician, who, with sparkling eyes, joyfully participates in creation.

We often receive letters asking the same question: "Have I applied the technique correctly?"

In response, we suggest this world view: *Everything that I do, I do in the best possible way.*

This is a phrase from that Bible of magicians *Between Two Chairs* by Evgeny Kliuev. The book's heroes, Ruler of the Word and the Show Queen, declare to Peterpaul, who embodies the common world view:

RULES MAY BE MADE UP
IN THE MIDDLE OF THE GAME!

Magical stories*

"I can't believe *that*!" said Alice... "One *can't* believe impossible things."

"I daresay you haven't had much practice," said the Queen. "When I was your age, I always did it for half-an-hour a day. Why, sometimes I've believed as many as six impossible things before breakfast."

Lewis Carroll—*Alice through the Looking Glass*

* Some of these stories were written from the perspective of the authors, Beard and Papa. Most of the names of people have been changed, and the names of many cities have been switched to Uriupinsk.

Magical family therapy

Letting go of being single

"Yes, my child!" Goodwin sighed, "You know, no one—literally no one in the world—knows what I am: The Great Deceiver. For how many years have I tricked, hid from, and in every possible way hoodwinked everyone around me. And you know, it's not so easy to be always pulling the wool over people's eyes."

Alexander Volkov—*The Wizard of the Emerald City*

I once had a client, a young woman, who wasn't able to sort out her personal life. Sighing mournfully, Katya complained that she was cursed by fate. It wasn't that she was physically unattractive or painfully shy. On the contrary, while speaking with her I noticed appreciatively her slender figure, her enchanting face with its large, chestnut eyes, her deep, resonant voice, open heart, and good taste in clothes.

She had plenty of admirers, too, but whenever a relationship would begin to become serious, they would just vanish into thin air. Each time that Katya met yet another young man, they would go out on dates together, have fun at parties, and gradually begin to develop a mutual affection toward each other. Then all of a sudden, without an argument or even an explanation, her boyfriend would simply disappear without a trace. Usually she found out later that he was an alcoholic, drug addict, or had a criminal record. "In the end," Katya admits, "every boyfriend I've ever had turned out to be the 'scum of society,' but you would never know it by looking at him." Over the past year, she had had no relationships at all.

Katya had already given up all hope of ever hearing the celebratory sounds of Mendelssohn's *Wedding March*, but then her friends told her that in Moscow there was a very unusual and joyful school of magicians, and she came to meet us. I briefly explained to her how magicians become liberated from life's problems.

In the process of examining her life, Katya and I discovered that, whenever yet another boyfriend disappeared, she was stricken by grief and despair. Katya had experienced such feelings throughout her life, long before her relationships with men. She traced these feelings back to early childhood. The relationship between her father and mother had been a difficult one. Her father drank heavily and left the family when Katya was still a young child. In the process of our work together, Katya gradually began to remember various incidents when she had felt very lonely and unwanted, and we finally uncovered the root episode.

It was winter, late in the evening, and a snow storm was howling outside. Little Katya was lying in her bed. Bright light streamed through the crack under her door. The sound of music, the clatter of plates and glasses, the lively voices and laughter of guests could be heard in the next room. Katya loved guests, and she couldn't fall asleep. She desperately wanted to go into the next room where it was all so exciting. Finally, the temptation was too great, and she surrendered to it. She called out loudly to her mother, who came in furious. Katya was bothering her at the height of the party. She lit into Katya, demanding that she be good and go to sleep. The tears and complaints of the little girl made her mother even angrier, and she ran out, slamming the door behind her. Katya was left in her room, dark and empty, rejected and alone in her cold bed. For perhaps the first time in her life, she felt utter loneliness and disappointment. She broke down completely, sobbing passionately into her pillow, and could not fall asleep for a long time.

What happened to Katya was not accidental. Evidently, her mother herself was lacking in warmth and emotional balance (despite the merriment of the party). Otherwise, she would not have treated her daughter in this way. The significance of this experience was that Katya needed to send a backdated gift of emotional well-being to her mother.

Katya remembered a time when she had felt deep gratitude toward her mother. One night, they were sitting snuggling together on Katya's little bed while her mother read *The Wizard of Oz* out loud to her. At that moment, they were completely content, and Katya felt incredible love and appreciation for her mother. In order to fix this memory in her being, a name was chosen for Katya: "I am the one who listens to mommy read *The Wizard of Oz*." This replaced the former name: "I am the one who is sobbing into my pillow, rejected by my mother." I advised Katya to repeat her new name often in order to change the events related with feelings of rejection and loneliness, and this would help her resolve her problems in relationships.

When she mentioned *The Wizard of Oz*, I instantly felt that the name chosen was perfect, that we were, in fact, on the right track. As a child I read and re-read this book many times over, and had often walked in my imagination along the yellow brick road. It was definitely an excellent support signal.

Recently, drawn by curiosity, I re-read the book and, to my utter delight, realized that it is actually all about *us*. Just look at the qualities the characters were seeking. The amusing Scarecrow dreamed of acquiring brains, although he was by no means a fool, and at times his wisdom even rescued his friends from difficulty. The Tin Woodsman longed for a genuine heart, but even without one he was capable of true love. And the Lion, who considered himself a coward, under pressure showed amazing bravery and courage.

However, what did the Great and Terrible Wizard of Oz (who in reality was a humble man from Nebraska) do to fulfill their dreams? Being an observant man, he noticed that these friends already possessed the qualities which they longed for, but the spectacle had to be played out fully. Therefore, the Great Humbug solemnly gave the Scarecrow a brain (a sack of bran mixed with pins and needles), the Tin Man a silk heart stuffed with sawdust, and the Lion drank down a goblet filled with "courage." The friends were overwhelmed with joy. Their dreams had come true!

Is this scene familiar? In order to resolve problems or fulfill a cherished wish, we need theater. There are many styles of theater—i.e., world views—just as the Wizard of Oz appeared to the travelers in various disguises: as a talking head, a beautiful woman, a ball of fire. Magicians easily, in good humor, switch one mask for another, remembering that in the end all world views are illusory. Our potential is limitless! But like the Cowardly Lion, we separate ourselves from what's truly possible by our dogged belief in the common world view.

In the course of my conversations with Katya, we encountered yet another issue—her conflict with her father. He lived alone, still drinking, and when he was drunk, he often telephoned Katya to berate her mercilessly. Furthermore, he was extremely troubled that she was not yet married.

"Daddy" was also renamed. His diagnostic name* sounded like this: "I am the one who persecutes and abuses Katya." This was changed to: "I am the one who opens a chest filled with precious stones." Katya pictured a gigantic wooden chest with rusty, iron bands around it locked by a heavy padlock. Suddenly, the padlock falls off, and the lid of the chest slowly creaks open. A miracle! Dazzling light shines from within. It is filled to the top with precious stones of every hue.

As I am writing these words, I recall that, in the room where I counseled Katya, there now stands a huge chest wrapped with iron bands (true, it lacks the precious stones). Now that is materialization!

Katya tried on her new masks with enthusiasm. Whenever she thought of her father, or was in direct contact with him, she repeated inwardly: "I am the one who opens a chest filled with precious stones." Her father stopped bothering her so much. When he did call, he was almost sober, asking how she was doing, and in general behaving himself. Her private life also began to improve. Not long after, Katya met an interesting young man. He liked her very much, and their relationship began to grow more serious. It seemed that the long-awaited wedding was finally approaching, but life was preparing yet another test for her.

She received an invitation to her brother's wedding. At first she didn't want to attend, since she had a bad feeling that her father would get smashed and make some kind of scene. But, in the end, Katya decided to go. When she arrived at the wedding, her father sarcastically asked her: "And when will we be celebrating *your* wedding?" He quickly slipped into his former pattern of behavior, standing up and proclaiming

* In the future we will omit diagnostic names easily established by context.

loudly: "It seems that I won't live long enough to see Katya's wedding! What's with you, Katya? Don't you respect your father? Did I bring you up to become so worthless that no one will marry you? Here I've been dreaming about having grandchildren to look after!"

She was thrown completely off track, and started getting massive headaches. On top of everything else, her boyfriend once again disappeared. Katya tried without success to reach him by telephone, but nobody was able to tell her where he was. For several months, she was overcome by weakness and apathy. Finally reaching her limit, she came to see me.

After examining the situation, Katya realized that she had switched back to her old world view, completely forgetting that she was a magician. She could have dealt with the situation in various ways: by thanking her father, opening the chest with precious stones, giving him a new name—for instance, "I am the one who looks after my grandchildren"—or many other options.

Father, who had played such a fateful role, was again renamed, although she could have continued to use the previous one if she had wanted. Her brother's new wife had just given birth to a son, and Katya's father was ecstatic. He constantly played with the baby, calling out in his joy: "At last I have a grandson! Now I can cook him applesauce!" The process of making applesauce for his grandson seemed very important to him. Hearing this, I couldn't resist giving him the appealing name: "I am the one who makes applesauce for my grandson." The image of mommy reading *The Wizard of Oz* was retained.

A few days later, Katya met a new prospect, and he was completely enamored by her. After that, I did not see her for about a year. However, recently I called her, and she announced proudly: "We got married six months ago. I'm so happy! Thank you so much for helping!"

We arranged a meeting on the following day at the subway station, so I could write down the details of her story. Katya arrived with a well-dressed, sturdily-built man and shyly introduced him. When I asked her how the applesauce was cooking, she told me that her father had come to her wedding and generously offered to buy them a new refrigerator. During our conversation, I noticed how Katya's husband carefully picked off a bit of lint from her cloak.

THE UNFAITHFUL HUSBAND

It was summer. On a warm, sunny morning, I set out for a lake located in a park not far from my home. I swim there all year round. There is a trailer near the lake where crowbars and shovels are kept to cut a hole in the ice during the winter. There are also shelves, clothes hangers, and at one time, as old timers will tell you, a woodstove. In hard frosts, especially during a strong wind, I change clothes in this trailer. Of course, the ice-hole is made right in front of the shed. Out of habit we also swim there in the summer.

On a tall birch tree near the trailer lives a family of crows. I made friends with this family, bringing leftovers to them every day—bits of cheese, sausage, fish entrails, chicken bones, or sometimes just stale bread crusts. Every morning the crow family dispatches a scout to meet me at the entrance to the park. This is my escort, flying from branch to branch alongside me. As I jog up to the trailer, the scout caws to notify his fellows that I have arrived, and answering calls are heard from every direction. These are the calls of scouts from other families who also know me well. A mass of crows is suddenly circling around me.

I sprinkle out the contents of my plastic bag onto a large stone, and the show begins. The hosts of the territory, who live in the nearest birch tree, try to drive away their uninvited guests, but there are so many that it is impossible to keep track of them all. In a frenzy, the hosts hurriedly try to stuff the contents of the bag into secret hiding places, but their neighbors swoop down from all directions, trying to steal the tasty morsels. All this is accompanied by a deafening din of crow curses. Every once in a while, I forget to bring food to the crows, and then, while I swim, the father of the family ransacks my belongings, searching for the cherished plastic bag. Once he stole my underpants and flew away with them. Only with difficulty did I manage to persuade him to give them back to me. After my swim, as I jog home, the father of the family always escorts me back to the park entrance.

On this particular morning, right before I set out for the lake, the telephone rang. It was an old friend, Svetlana. Sobbing bitterly, she explained to me that her husband had cheated on her. When he told her, Svetlana gathered up all his belongings and threw him out of the house. But now she regretted it. He had just left town on a business trip, and she asked me to help her sort out the situation.

I told her that I would come to see her after I went swimming, did my exercises, and fed the crows. Completing my morning ritual, I performed a special dance* in thanks for the coming day. I often do this when I have a "complicated" day ahead of me. Dancing in nature is especially powerful. Barefooted and in my swimsuit, I danced on the soft grass covered over with translucent drops of dew. At the end, I received the mantra TIRABANDA and, filled with inspiration, jogged home. I then practiced yoga for an hour, cooked buckwheat

---

* The dancer performs spontaneous movements with closed eyes, speaking words in gibberish. Sometimes the speech of the dancer may sound like a foreign language. Often the dancer sings as well, composing a melody while dancing. The gibberish and the tune, tempo and rhythm of the melody may change several times during a single dance. The performer can also envision pictures in his imagination. The magical dance ends with a final movement and a word in gibberish— the mantra.

porridge for breakfast, and sat down to enjoy it in thoughtful contemplation. Only when all this was done did I set off for Svetlana's apartment, repeating the mantra along the way.

Svetlana greeted me with tears. At first, she appealed to my sense of justice and tried to provoke me into condemning her husband, but I didn't fall for it. To prepare Svetlana for constructive work, I told her several stories about magicians. When I had managed to bring her to a point when she could think straight, I suggested that she search her childhood for the root of the situation. Svetlana declared confidently that nothing like this had ever happened to her in her life. We then began to analyze her relationships with men.

After prolonged work, Svetlana finally remembered the root episode. At the age of three and a half, she fell in love with a little boy named Vova in nursery school, but he preferred another girl. At home, Svetlana went into hysterics. She gathered up all her favorite toys, brought them to the nursery school the next day, and performed a "wedding" for Vova and her rival.

To deal with this root experience, Svetlana first gave thanks to Vova: "Thank you, Vova, for warning me that 'love triangles'—when I love a man but he loves another—may occur repeatedly in my life. I could react by throwing out the one I love, and my life will become a never-ending search for the perfect man."

Svetlana next recalled a time when she had given Vova self-confidence and emotional comfort. It was at a May Day celebration. The hall in the nursery school was beautifully decorated, with strings of colorful pennants stretched from wall to wall. Girls were wearing light pastel dresses, and the boys wore white shirts with black shorts; everyone was wearing the obligatory knee-length white socks. The nursery school

teachers also were dressed up for the occasion, holding bou-
quets of beautiful flowers, and children carried around flags
and balloons. The sunlight streaming in through the windows
reflected brightly on the polished parquet floor. The atmosphere was joyful and festive, charged with excitement. Svetlana was dancing with Vova in the middle of the hall. The
dance ended, and everyone clapped with delight. Svetlana and
Vova were presented with gifts, and Vova was very happy.

Svetlana conceived her magical name: *"I am the one who
dances with Vova at the May Day celebration."* Her face began
shining and her cheeks flushed. She was still dancing with
Vova in nursery school.

I have a personal criterion for gauging the quality of my
work. When done brilliantly, a hot wave of energy begins at
the top of my head, descends to the base of my spine, and then
continues through my legs and feet into the ground. I even
sometimes feel myself physically lighter. I experienced this
feeling when Svetlana remembered her dance with Vova.

Over the next three hours, Svetlana and I drank tea together, and she told me a delightful story, which I have since
often used in my work with clients. It was a story about when
Svetlana took her daughter Natasha to nursery school for the
first time. This is usually a highly emotional time for a child.
Many children will cry for the first several days but eventually become resigned, even resentful. Often this resentment
remains with them throughout their lives.

Svetlana thought up an amazing ritual for the occasion.
She invited her parents and friends to her apartment on the
evening before Natasha's first day and prepared a sumptuous
meal. The party was dedicated to Natasha and everyone came
with gifts. The guests offered numerous toasts to Natasha,
congratulating her for being so grown-up as to go to nursery
school. There would be many children there who would be

fun to play with; and if adults have to go to work, than children must go to nursery school. There were so many gifts that they filled a huge cardboard box in the living room.

The spectacle didn't end there. The next day Svetlana took Natasha to her new school and arranged a special ritual with the teacher. All the children lined up, and one by one they were introduced to the new girl. Natasha approached each child, greeted them, and gave them a chocolate candy. Afterwards, the children played *Rucheyok.**

Smiling, Svetlana told me that sometimes, especially those first few days, she could clearly see on Natasha's face that she didn't want to go off to school. But could she really let down the adults who had believed in her? So she went to nursery school without a murmur, and I can say with certainty that she didn't shed a single tear. The entire ritual was a way to rename Natasha as *"the one who treats children to candy and plays games with them."*

Before leaving, I explained to Svetlana that, in order to unravel her situation, it was enough simply to remember her dance with Vova. When her husband returned from his business trip, their relationship was renewed, and for the past several years contentment and well-being have reigned in their family.

---

* *Rucheyok* (Russian for "little stream")—an ancient game played to find your intended mate. Pairs of young people stand in a double line, holding each other by the hand and raising them up high to form a long arch. A person without a partner starts from one end and passes through the arch, on the way choosing and taking along a mate; this new couple takes their place at the end of the line. The person left without a partner goes to the head of the line and passes through the arch to choose a new mate; and the "stream" keeps flowing forward. [trans]

LOVE RESTORED

Nikolay was around forty years old—an intelligent, likable, good-looking fellow. Therefore, his problem was quite unexpected. Nikolay told me that not once in his life had he truly loved a woman. It's not that women were not interested in him. He even believed that there were a few women, including his wife, who loved him dearly, but Nikolay considered women as silly creatures meant only for sex, which he liked very much. However, now he felt that he was missing something very important.

In this case, the technique of searching for the root experience seemed most appropriate. Little by little, we probed deeply into Nikolay's past, until finally we uncovered an underlying episode from his life.

When I was in sixth grade, a new girl came to our school. Her name was Vera, and I liked her straight off. I remember her two little braids, her lacey, white cuffs, and her enormous eyes. She was also a very good student. She was growing into a very beautiful girl, with well-developed breasts and slender legs. I knew that the other boys in my class were attracted to her as well. One day, Vera's friend, Lena, stopped me in the school corridor. With a conspiratorial look, she handed me a neatly folded note, in which Vera confessed her eternal love for me.

A wave of emotion overwhelmed me, an exhilarating joy that Vera—so desirable and at the same time so inaccessible—was now nervously awaiting my reply. On the other hand, I also experienced fear, because Lena knew Vera's secret. I believed that Lena, whom I considered a sneak, also liked me. If I made a date with Vera, then Lena might tell everyone, and the boys would tease us.

So there were two movies playing in my mind. In one, I was on a date with Vera. We went out to the movies, bought ice-cream, and kissed.

In the second movie, our classmates in their envy were making fun of us. They wouldn't leave us alone, especially Danny. Danny and I had been friends since the first grade, but at the same time we were always rivals competing to be the leader. I was the best student and soccer player, but he could run faster than me, hung out with the cool crowd, and had taken up smoking and drinking. Danny also liked Vera. Knowing his way of making the most of any situation, I imagined how his revenge would turn to bullying. I would lose Danny's friendship, and along with it my status among my peers.

In the end, fear won out, and I did a cruel thing. That evening at home, I was reading a humor magazine and saw the following poem:

> "I'll be friends with anyone,"
> Said tar stuck on a shoe.
> It didn't know the shoe despised
> Being smeared with goo!

The following day at school, I showed Vera's letter to the gang of boys led by Danny. Then I read to them the poem about tar and sent it to Vera. For long the boys laughed with malicious joy. My status was raised, but even now I suffer from pangs of remorse for my behavior.

This was clearly not the root episode, so Nikolay continued uncovering memories. In the first grade he also had been handed a love note, and for some reason had felt ashamed of it. Where did this shame come from? At last Nikolay reached the root experience.

I was about four years old and in nursery school. Our teacher had a two-year-old daughter, Masha, who was a charming little girl, very much like a doll. In fact, for the children she was a living doll, and we loved to play with her. I liked Masha very much. I especially enjoyed helping her get dressed before we went out for a walk, putting on her coat and tying her shoelaces. I vividly recall her red coat and hood. They were made of a very soft material, which reminded me of the plush sofa in my grandmother's room. I loved lying on that sofa; it felt as if the soft velvet was tenderly caressing my skin.

Once when we were getting ready to go out, my father, whom I adored, arrived at the school. He saw how I helped Masha get ready and laughed loudly: "Hey, look at those two! The bride and groom!" A feeling of shame cut through me like a knife. "I must be doing something wrong," I thought.

Nikolay felt a lump rise in his throat, and his eyes became moist. He was that four-year-old boy again, and he could hardly keep back his tears. Nikolay realized that his present attitude toward women was conceived at that very moment. Little Nicky had misunderstood his daddy's laughter. The boy had thought that the feelings which he had toward Masha were something to be ashamed of, deserving of ridicule. And Nikolay had continued to mock those feelings for over thirty-five years. Renaming him was easy: *"I am the one who is helping Masha put on her plush coat."* In fact, in this case it wasn't even necessary to repeat the name. It was enough for him to recall his pure feelings toward Masha, even to just remember her.

Nikolay called me a few months later. He was overjoyed to report that he had at last found the true love which his heart had so longed for.

THIS IS NO WAY TO TREAT A PREGNANT WOMAN!

Zhenya had married for the second time. She was happy with her new husband and was soon expecting a child. However, they unexpectedly started arguing, and one day he suddenly left home without an explanation. He didn't come back, he didn't call, and Zhenya had no idea what had happened to him. She was extremely resentful, and the thought haunted her relentlessly: "Why did he do this to me? *This is no way to treat a pregnant woman!*" She couldn't sleep, and her blood pressure plunged to a critical level. After fainting several times, she finally had to go to the hospital.

When she came to us, we decided to use the method of searching for the root. To begin, we told her stories about other people who had searched for the root episode in order to rename themselves. First Papa related the story of Lena.

Our Department Head was not only a dull man, but also very belligerent. Maybe he was belligerent because he was dull, or maybe he was just born that way. It was not surprising that he had to have an ulcer treated twice a year. The situation in the Department was intolerable, but all the employees kept silent for fear of retaliation. I had only a short time until retirement, but had finally reached the end of my rope. I told him exactly what I thought of him—let him fire me!

Almost immediately after this scene, I attended a magician's seminar and, when they explained the technique of renaming by searching for the root, I decided to apply it to resolve this conflict. As a result of my search, I remembered something which had happened to me when I was three or four years old during the Second World War. I was attending nursery school. We didn't like our nursery school teachers and were afraid of them, since they were very strict and cold toward us. They were affectionate and pleasant only to the "rich kids" from families of army officers, KGB* officers, and doctors. These parents would give the teachers extra ration cards and boxes of candy. It was a boarding school, and the privileged children were given chocolate on the sly, but we knew about it. Once somebody stole a piece of chocolate, causing massive searches and investigations.

Feelings of injustice, prejudice, and humiliation always remained fixed in my memory, but there were also many bright moments. The most precious to me were music lessons, the children's choir, and piano. I found the name: *"I am the one who is singing in the choir,"* sending joy to my former nursery school teachers. I sing specifically to them, to their honor and glory.

The name worked right away; it instilled in me a deep inner peace. Conflicts with my boss have ceased completely over the last year and a half. All our former issues were settled easily and peacefully. But the most unexpected surprise was the bouquet of flowers he presented to me on my birthday!

The narration was then continued by Beard:

Once a young woman named Liza came to me for advice. Crying bitterly, she told me her tale of unhappy love.

* Soviet Secret Police. [trans]

She had fallen madly in love with a man who, in the beginning, had reciprocated her feelings. Liza had very interesting work in a reputable firm, and the man she fell in love with was the firm's director. Of course, many of her colleagues knew that Liza was having an affair at work. Her life was exciting and fulfilling, but then in a single moment everything fell apart.

Suddenly, without any explanation, her lover started avoiding her. When he heard Liza's voice on the telephone, he quickly hung up the receiver. Although they still had to see each other at work, the director was deliberately cool and official, letting her know that everything was finished between them. Soon she realized that some "well-wisher" had whispered to her boss goodness knows what about her. Everywhere at work she could feel the mocking glances of her colleagues, and when she wasn't invited to his birthday party, she fell into a state of despair. Liza suffered from loneliness and deeply resented him for dumping her.

We discovered that her relationships with men were always accompanied by similar feelings. She had experienced such feelings a few years before when her husband had left her, and even earlier, in the eighth grade, when her first love, Misha, had unexpectedly cut her off. The reason for that split was because one of his friends had told him that Liza was kissing someone else.

In order to properly rename herself, we suggested to Liza that she search for a time when she had given Misha happiness and emotional warmth. Once, when they were walking hand in hand in silence through the woods, the autumn leaves rustling beneath their feet, she remembered her profound feelings of love and gratitude toward Misha. From "the one who is suffering the loss of her sweetheart," she became *"the one who is walking hand in hand with Misha through the autumn woods."*

It was a true transformation. Instead of crying and being the "persecuted martyr," she transformed right in front of me into a woman full of life with sparkling eyes, excitedly telling me how she felt as if a mountain had fallen from her shoulders.

It was obvious that the split with Misha was far from her first, primary episode of feelings of loss and loneliness. Liza admitted that even when that relationship was going well, she was occasionally overwhelmed by some vague fear. She was afraid that somehow their love would suddenly vanish, but she couldn't *recall* any earlier episode to base this on. In order to help Liza find the root episode, I (Beard) told her a story from my own life.

Once I decided to sort out a personal issue—my longtime habit of taking offense at people or situations which treated me "wrongly" or "unfairly." I was riding the subway, relaxing with my eyes closed. I began with the last time I had become offended and, maintaining this feeling in myself, slipped down through a chain of events into the past. At a certain point, I came to a stop, feeling that I couldn't remember any relevant event further back. I quit straining my memory and *simply relaxed*.

Suddenly, as if in slow-motion, I saw myself off to one side, a tiny baby, probably about one year old. My Auntie was carrying me, wrapped up in a green blanket. She was descending the stairs, but suddenly tripped and dropped me. I fell down hard onto the stairs and began screaming wildly, not so much from pain, but rather from fear and indignation: Why did I deserve this?!

How could I rename myself? I skipped back a little to the moment when, without a care, I lay peacefully in my Auntie's arms. Suddenly I realized that I was looking at the world through the eyes of that tiny baby. The world looked so completely different—bright and wonderful! The ceiling, the walls, the banisters—everything was sprinkled over with shining sparkles, like snowflakes dancing in the light of a street lamp. The space all around me was not in a fixed form; it seemed to be breathing.

How long did I remain in this state? Probably just a few seconds, and then it slipped away, leaving only the slight trace of a memory. But even this was enough to experience an amazing feeling of liberation, as if returning to a marvelous source of joy within me. Now, whenever I become upset by that familiar feeling of resentment, I simply remember that brief enchanting moment of early childhood.

No sooner had I finished this story than Liza exclaimed with excitement:

I remember! I was three years old, and my daddy, whom I adored, was pulling me on a sled in our park. The snow was crunching under his boots, and the sun was shining brightly. Huge mounds of snow sparkled with every color of the rainbow. Then all of a sudden the whole world went dim. The feeling of happiness was changed first into astonishment, and then into an icy terror: "Where's daddy? He's not here, and I'm all alone in this strange place! He'll probably never come back!" I cried out with all the anguish of my heart. As it turned out, he was just playing a game with me. He had tied up the sled and was hiding behind a tree. Fascinated by the sparkling colors, I hadn't noticed him sneak off. It was the first real shock in my life triggered by the loss of a loved one. Despite the fact that he instantly came out of hiding as soon as he heard my screams, the fear of losing someone dear to me has always dwelt in me since that time.

After this seemingly innocent episode, Liza began transmitting fear and expectation of loss into the world around her throughout her life. She gladly agreed to try to change this old pattern. Returning in her imagination to the walk in the park, Liza suggested to her daddy that they play snowballs together. Instead of the diagnostic name: "I am the one who became very frightened when Daddy hid," Liza acquired a new name: *"I am the one who plays snowballs with Daddy."*

Six months later, I crossed paths with Liza once more at a magician's seminar. Much had changed in her life. She declared that she had found a deep, inner peace. When I asked whether her "prodigal Director" had returned to her, Liza flippantly replied: "What do I need him for?"

Finally, Zhenya could not take the pressure anymore and *remembered* a scene from her childhood:

It was winter. I was about three years old and sick with the mumps. Because my mother was a dedicated young communist, her work was more important to her than me, and she left me at home alone, telling herself that I was old enough. She asked a neighbor who lived three stories below us to occasionally check in on me. Two hours passed and I began to feel sorry for myself, because mommy had left me all alone, and my ear was aching. I started crying, and angry thoughts swirled through my mind: *"This is no way to treat a sick child!"* I began screaming, so that someone would hear me and realize that a poor, innocent child was all alone, terrified and miserable. But no one heard me, and no one came to comfort me. Suddenly I realized that I would be better off going to nursery school, which I disliked, than to be sick at home all alone. Soon after that I recovered.

Based on our experience with other clients, we felt that even this was not the root episode. To search for the root, we had to use the key phrases: *"This is no way to treat a pregnant woman!"* and *"This is no way to treat a sick child!"* Zhenya turned out to be a talented patient. We were working in her home, and suddenly, with shining eyes and flushed cheeks, she jumped up and ran into another room, returning with a family photo album. Thumbing through the album, she *recalled* a whole series of episodes, including the root one.

I was very little, and it was a dark night. We were with an army unit in the forest on the border between Austria and Hungary (my father was a military man). I woke up and discovered that I was alone in the room. There was a terrifying silence all around me. I felt a lump in my throat, and tearfully said to myself: *"This is no way to treat a young child!"* I crawled out of bed and thought that my parents probably didn't even know that I had learned how to get out of bed by myself. I got dressed, opened the door, and went outside. I quietly sneaked past the sleeping guard and walked along a dimly lit gravel road through some oak trees to the dining hall, which was quite far from our cabin. I was terribly frightened. A single thought kept desperately circling my mind: "I will get there no matter what, just to spite them! Let them be ashamed! After all, they abandoned me, which is no way to treat a young child!"

At last I reached the dining hall and found my mother, who was baking bread rolls for breakfast. Mother gasped with surprise and outrage. Her face reflected questions which had no answers: "How could she get out of bed, walk past the guard, and come here all by herself?" The only thing my mother could think of doing was to give me a piece of dough and let me stay with her until morning, shaping bread rolls. I had difficulty forming the rolls because the dough kept breaking apart, and I kept trying to pinch the dough back together. In the end, one of my rolls did manage to make it onto the baking tray.

Renaming Zhenya was easy. Instead of the diagnostic name: "I am a pregnant woman abandoned by my husband, and this is no way to treat a pregnant woman!" a more effective name was chosen: "I am the one who crawls out of bed, sneaks past the guard, and walks through the forest to bake bread rolls with mommy." For convenience we shortened it to: *"I am the one who walks through the forest."*

It was summertime and a few days later we went to the annual Summer Solstice Gathering. When we returned two weeks later, we found that Zhenya had begun an extensive renovation of her apartment. It looked like it had sustained a direct hit by an artillery shell. She even had to redo part of the outer brickwork of her nine-story building. From early morning until late at night, she was busy purchasing building materials and furniture. Although her husband still hadn't returned, there was not a trace of depression left in her. On the contrary, Zhenya was resolute and, even as she was making all these repairs, she decided to begin writing her dissertation.

NEW YEAR'S EVE DANCE OR HOW TO BECOME A SHAMAN

But the fun's not getting into trouble, it's getting out. The game is to remember who we are, and use our power tools... We experiment... to make our outer world reflect our inner... And when it changes once, three times, ten, we grow a little bolder and sure enough, the tools work! With practice we trust them utterly.

Richard Bach—*Running from Safety*

The room was permeated by the fragrant smell of fir branches set in a large, crystal vase and decorated with bright, colorful ornaments. On the television I heard the immortal line of the inebriated Ippolit: "This jellied fish is absolutely horrible!"* My wife, Lenulia, was bustling about the kitchen. I, too, was busy, carrying dishes from the kitchen to the holiday table, occasionally snatching on the run a crunchy cucumber or a marinated mushroom.

These New Year's Eve preparations were suddenly interrupted by a telephone call from my wife's friend, Olga. She urgently begged us to rescue her from her drunk husband,

---

* A famous quote from a classical 1975 Soviet movie *The Irony of Fate, or Have a Nice Sauna* directed by Eldar Riazanov. The movie tells the story of a doctor, who on a New Year's Eve accidentally finds himself in a distant city where he meets the woman of his dreams. This comedy has been a long-time Russian favorite and is traditionally aired on December 31st. [trans]

who was cursing and threatening her while trying to break down the locked bedroom door. The prospect of missing the holiday festivities to drive to the other end of the world to pacify Olga's enraged husband was not attractive at all. Magicians, in general, are a lazy lot.

I instructed Olga to calm down and wait for a favorable resolution to the conflict. I was going to work with this problem using a new method—the magician's dance.

Tuning inwardly into the situation, I began to dance. To an uninitiated spectator, it would have appeared extremely exotic, at times even like a shaman's dance. The body of the dancer moves spontaneously and may twist into very unusual positions. In addition, the dance is accompanied by a very original sound track—howling, or melodic singing, or a loud, vibrating sound. Lenulia was seeing the dance for the first time; at first she was somewhat surprised and only just managed to keep from giggling. When I finally froze on one foot, in a posture reminiscent of a swallow, or maybe a frog with outstretched legs, Lenulia's verdict was short but definite: "Kashchenko!"* She returned to the kitchen reassured. I felt that the work had been performed well, since I could feel a fresh surge of energy and was in a state of inner peace and serenity.

Soon the incident was forgotten. It was not until three o'clock in the morning that my wife finally called Olga back to find out how things were going. In complete astonishment, Olga told her that, right after their previous conversation, Olga's husband had suddenly calmed down. What's more, he even apologized for his horrible behavior and begged her forgiveness. Peace was restored between them, and they brought in the New Year together. But the influence of the magical

---

* Kashchenko is a name for a famous Moscow psychiatric clinic. [trans]

dance had an even more far-reaching effect. Two weeks later, we found out from Olga that since that night her husband had not touched a single drop of alcohol.

Even I, who had already begun to get used to such miraculous events, did not expect such a sudden turnaround. Really, though, there is nothing fantastic about this story at all. Simply by performing a "shaman's dance," I had *allowed myself* to deal with various complex, problematical situations.

METAMORPHOSIS

Before our wedding, my mother-in-law, Isabella Matveevna,* was always nice to me. She was welcoming, kind, and always interested in how I was doing, how things were going at work. Whenever she saw me, she would treat me to tea, lingonberry pie, and her homemade quince jam, and she generously gave me presents on every occasion.

Then, only two days after the wedding, Isabella Matveevna transformed into a completely different person. That day I came home from school (I am a teacher) to a deathly silence. My mother-in-law did not even come out of her room. Perplexed, I went into the kitchen to cook dinner. When she heard the clatter of dishes, she came out and stood motionless in the doorway, not even saying hello. I asked her what I should prepare. With a distorted face, she mumbled: "I couldn't care less. Whatever crap you like to eat!" She turned and went away. A dark time began in my life.

My mother-in-law had changed beyond recognition. Where had her kindness, her smile disappeared to? She stopped acknowledging me, and never left her room; nor did she greet me or ask about anything. If I came to her room to offer help, Isabella rudely drove me away: "Get out of here! I

---

* *Matveevna* is Isabella's patronymic derived from her father's name Matvey. Addressing a person by her first name and patronymic conveys a respectful attitude, or the superiority of that person in status or age. This story is narrated by a young woman. [trans]

103

don't need anything. I can take care of myself." I cooked better than her, and this made her jealous. If my father-in-law complimented my culinary skill, I knew I was in for another storm. Once Isabella Matveevna declared to me with a spiteful smile: "At work, the women have noticed that lately I've been coming to their office for tea. They say that my daughter-in-law is eating me out of house and home." This hit me very hard, especially since my husband and I were paying for all the food, and I did most of the cooking.

My attempts to settle the conflict went nowhere. If I even approached Isabella Matveevna, she would turn and walk away. I was afraid to go into her room for fear of abuse. She would tell her son that everything was fine, and in his presence she behaved as she had before our wedding. I asked my husband what was going on, but he didn't want to get involved. "If I see something happen, I'll speak to mother about it. Otherwise, there's nothing I can do until I have some kind of evidence."

It was a dead-end situation. I had no idea what to do and cried for hours in despair. I lost interest in everything. After work, I waited at the school until my husband had left work, and only then went home. My only desire was to move out of the apartment. Whenever I saw Isabella in her sweater and sweatpants, with her tight bun of gray hair, and the cold reflection in her glasses, an icy shudder would pass through me. I was on the edge of a nervous breakdown. I couldn't sleep at night, and my thoughts tormented me—at work, on the bus, in stores. This nightmare lasted for about six months.

Then I met this magician who taught me the technique of thanksgiving. I thanked Isabella for warning me that I may have to run away from home to God knows where. I brought her a gift of joy, tranquility, and good relationships with people. For the next two days, in response to her attacks,

I rewarded my mother-in-law with imaginary gifts—a basket of exotic flowers, stylish party dresses and luxurious lingerie, pre-Revolutionary tins of fruit drops, a food processor with artificial intelligence, and so on. I began to feel a deep inner peace and glimmer of hope for my situation.

On the third day something extraordinary occurred. I returned home from work and Isabella stepped out of the doorway of her lair, asking if I wanted something to eat. I was dumbstruck. I hadn't even taken off my coat when she came straight up to me with those quick little steps in her knitted slippers, holding up a flowerpot. Among the long, prickly leaves bloomed a cluster of large, purple flowers. Isabella Matveevna could not restrain her joy: "Look! It's done nothing for so long, and now it's blooming! Look how beautiful it is!" It was the first time since I moved in that she had spoken to me when my husband wasn't in the room—the first swallow of spring.

After that, my mother-in-law was again kind and cordial toward me, and I no longer had to send her exotic gifts. Isabella now patiently tries to understand my various concerns. She gives me complete freedom in my cooking experiments, and never tires of praising them. Whatever I buy for the house—a sponge or a brush or anything—it always meets her approval. And God forbid that she should see me tidying up! She immediately stops me, saying: "Take a rest, my dear. You must be tired after your long day at work."

My husband is happy that I have become calmer and more attentive to him. And one last detail: every day my mother-in-law and I discuss the various soap operas. Although I'm not a passionate fan, she likes to keep me informed of the main events. I find out that Manuela has proclaimed her true love to Fernando, and that treacherous Raquel is once again up to her intrigues…

Down with English tests!

"Daddy, let's go buy new skis."
"I don't feel like it."
"But I've been doing magic!"
"OK, let's go then."

Conversation in a magician's family

Nastya, who is in grade school, attended a training seminar in magic and quickly mastered this ancient art. Children are born magicians; it is as natural as breathing to them.

Nastya was not especially diligent in her study of the English language, but only too soon she had to face her first test. Her mother was very concerned about it, because it had been difficult to get her daughter into her elite school. A bad grade on the English test would mean a very unpleasant conversation with her teacher.

Nastya had this choice: to study, or to resort to magic. A third option combining these two was rejected straight away, even though it could have yielded excellent results. It's not difficult to guess that the first option, which would require poring over textbooks, was not very attractive to Nastya.

Nastya gave thanks to her mother for warning her that her worries could come true, and Nastya could be kicked out of the school in disgrace. The girl imagined a gift for her mother in the form of a hedgehog with multi-colored marshmallows stuck onto the tips of its quills.

The hedgehog's endeavors were not in vain—the English examination was postponed three times. First, the English teacher had to leave for urgent business; next, the entire class was sent away for vaccinations; and then something else delayed the test. The main culprit of all this commotion, Nastya, gained much needed extra time—three whole weeks, in fact. If only she had used this extra time! But magicians tend to be lazy. In the end, the test was finally given, and Nastya got a "C" on it. Everyone was happy.

KARLSSON* AND THE LITTLE BLUE TOOLBOX

My son Andrey is in the eighth grade.** In years past, his report cards had shown mostly average grades. If I didn't remind him, he would completely forget about his homework. All my urging and punishments were useless.

I started thinking about what he was lacking and realized that throughout his childhood I had imposed my will too severely on him, limiting his creative abilities. I remembered how I had forced him to read his primer when learning to read. He would immediately become absent-minded and bored. It became clear that my son needed more freedom and independence. I began searching for a time when I had allowed Andrey to express his creativity.

At around four or five years old, Andrey had a favorite game. He would get his little blue toolbox out of the closet and take out the hammer, screwdrivers, and wood plane. Then he would begin making things—nothing all that special, in my opinion—but he enjoyed the process immensely. He would remove all the tools, lay them out onto the floor, and start

---

* Karlsson-on-the-Roof is a fictional character in a series of children's books written by Swedish author Astrid Lindgren which is very popular among Russian children. He is a very mischievous, stout little fellow with a propeller on his back and is the best at everything, at least according to himself. [trans]

** This story is narrated by a woman. [trans]

banging away. Sometimes he might hammer together a loose chair leg. So I renamed him: *"The one who hammers noisily."*

Two weeks passed, and Andrey's grades began to improve. He finished the second term with fantastic results—he got "B's" in history and literature, but the "B" in Russian language completely shocked me. In the past, he had always received "C's" in Russian. I didn't know what to expect next from my son. In the third term he received a "B" in physics, which also had never happened before. For his final lab work in physics, he even got an "A." I began to understand Andrey better and gave him more freedom. I gave him permission to travel to St. Petersburg with his class and stopped worrying when he came home late.

Besides his studies, I was concerned about yet another issue. When he was in the third and fourth grades, he used to read a lot, but after that books completely disappeared from his desk. He would hang around outside all day, and I never could convince him to read on his own. No doubt I pushed Andrey too hard here as well, forcing him to read books against his will. After much consideration, I decided to rename myself: *"I am the one who reads Andrey a book about Karlsson."* This was his favorite book when he was little. He always roared with laughter as he listened to the adventures of Karlsson and the little boy who was his friend. Andrey identified with Karlsson and chuckled with delight at Karlsson's comical description of himself: "I am a handsome, smart, and well-fed little man in the prime of my life!"

Andrey instantly began to devour books. In the last two months, he has read *The Three Musketeers*, *The Count of Monte Cristo*, and *Robinson Crusoe*. Recently, I noticed on his desk a book by Zoshchenko.*

---

* Mikhail Zoshchenko (1895-1958): a popular Russian writer of short humorous stories. [trans]

Stories of material success

An apartment and a cottage

It was April.* My friend's husband, Vova, was telling me about an interesting method of magic he practiced, but I really couldn't understand anything he said. I had to thank some Vanya, and miracles would begin to happen. At first, I just ignored him, but finally, intrigued by the success stories he related, I decided to try it out.

I turned to him: "You keep harping about this magical system. Alright then, I need an apartment in town and a cottage in the country. The cottage should be in the village Malakhovka** with natural gas and telephone service already hooked up. And the apartment should be a one-room flat in the Novogireevo District within a hundred meters of the subway station."

"Wow! You're asking for a lot," Vova replied, whistling. But he performed a dance and gave me the mantra CHI YORVA. He also taught me a magical gesture: you move your hands downwards outlining the shape of a large urn.

I chuckled inwardly, since I really didn't take any of this nonsense seriously. However, I nonetheless began repeating the mantra aloud and outlining the imaginary urn with my hands. I liked doing both. Whenever I was walking to my

---

* This story is narrated by a young woman. [trans]

** Located just outside the city limits of Moscow, Malakhovka has grown to be an elite—and very expensive—location for a summer cottage, or *dacha*. [trans]

friend's, who lived not far from me, I waved my arms and boldly chanted CHI YORVA despite the strange looks of people around me. Some felt sorry for me, others smiled, but I had a lot of fun with it. In time, the mantra became a part of me. Once Vova, smiling whimsically, advised me to write this mantra 108 times; this would make it even more powerful. So before going to bed that night, I took out a thick piece of paper and wrote CHI YORVA exactly 108 times. Then I pinned the paper onto the wall, where I could easily see it.

In August I went on vacation to Pitsunda, a resort on the Black Sea. One day, I called my mother to ask her how things were going at home. Hearing my voice, my mother burst out crying, and then started yelling, demanding something from me. It took me a while to finally understand that her sister, Varya (my aunt), with whom my mother had broken all contact twenty years before, had returned out of nowhere. We hadn't seen her or heard anything about her for all those years after their falling out.

Aunt Varya came to my mom and begged her to persuade me to accept her apartment as a gift. She was 75 years old and single. She had never had much love in her life, and nobody was taking care of her in her old age. She kept insisting impatiently that I end my vacation and return home immediately. Interestingly, my aunt's one-room flat included a large kitchen and balcony, and was located in a block of apartments directly in front of the Novogireevo subway station.

Logically speaking, my aunt should have left her apartment to her nephew, Georgy, who had grown up near her and was the only person whom she had ever loved and accepted. In general, Aunt Varya was a closed and suspicious person. She never had guests over, and her sympathy toward Georgy was shown only by the fact that she sometimes bought him slippers.

After the telephone conversation with my mother, I recalled how many times I had teased Vova: "So where's my apartment? And what about that cottage in Malakhovka? I still don't have enough money, so how will I get my apartment and cottage?"

Vova answered calmly: "It will definitely happen at some point, in 27. Just keep working on it."

I thought that 27 (of heaven knows what) was one of Vova's silly pranks. Then all of a sudden my aunt, who actually had strong moral principles but often came off rather harsh, had made this paradoxical decision to give me her apartment. None of the relatives had expected this. You would understand if you knew my aunt. She never threw anything away, not even empty matchboxes. She was worse than Scrooge. So I decided to forget about it and find out more when I returned to Moscow.

On the day that I was to arrive home, Aunt Varya came to our home at 8:00 in the morning and, by the time I finally got in at 3:00 that afternoon, she was on the brink of tears. She shouted to me from the doorway: "Do you want the apartment or not? Or are you going to make a fool out of me and keep dragging me along?"

I replied: "Hello, Aunt Varya! I'm so glad to see you. I've been trying to figure out what exactly you want; you know, I've never asked you for anything. Please give me a little time to think it over."

I tried my best to postpone making the decision, because I couldn't believe that my aunt's offer was genuine. But when I saw her a couple of months later, she burst into tears, chastising me for not wanting to help out an old woman. At last I yielded and started putting together the paperwork to transfer the apartment. During this time, my Aunt fell and hurt herself badly. Her doctor suspected that she had broken her hip which, considering her age, could have serious complications. I had to speed up the process, and I again turned to Vova for help seeing the paperwork through to the end.

This time Vova gave me a picture of a red carpet runner with green fringe stretched across a rye field. At the end of the carpet stood a huge oak desk. It was covered with a heavy green cloth with an elegant, bronze inkwell, blotting paper, a pen holder, and some contraption which was half-clock and half-compass.

Armed with this picture, I went to the appropriate government office to get the necessary certificate. When I arrived, though, I was shocked to find out that I had come on a day when they were closed to the public. A glum voice chided me from within: "Even if they were open, I probably won't get anything out of these bureaucrats. This kind of paperwork can take months to process, and today no one will even talk to me."

Women with piles of papers were scurrying from door to door. The receptionist windows, which normally have long lines of people in front of them, were securely shut. A feeling of hopelessness overcame me.

Suddenly, I heard loud shouts coming from behind a door with a nameplate reading: "Liudmila Vasilievna Groznaya,* Deputy Director." The door burst open, banging against the wall, and a sweaty, red-faced man dashed out. In one hand he held a pile of dog-eared documents; in the other a half-opened briefcase. A voice shouted after him: "Never bring

---

* In Russian, *Groznaya* actually means "Terrible," "Threatening," or "Formidable." This is also an epithet of the Russian tsar Ivan the Terrible (1530-1584), who is still remembered for his bloody repressions, wars, and moral corruption. Liudmila Groznaya's patronymic (Vasilievna) is also the same as that of Ivan the Terrible.

your documents to me in such a mess again! Sometimes I don't even sign documents which are submitted properly. And when you come see me, you must be clear about what you have and exactly what you need. You can't just expect to get whatever you want whenever you happen to show up. We are serious people here, with serious work to do."

The frightened man quickly disappeared down the corridor, and I unexpectedly found myself face-to-face with a nice-looking middle-aged woman who had suddenly appeared in the doorway. She had bleach-blond hair piled high on her head, knitted brows, heavy blue eye shadow, and bright red lipstick. She wore an elegant, gray suit, and her eyes radiated a managerial zeal.

Immediately I pictured the red carpet runner with green fringe, and imagined Liudmila Vasilievna herself sitting behind the gigantic oak desk. Then I turned to the real director, and her face became calm and welcoming. She said in a deep, even voice: "What do *you* want?"

I was speechless. Liudmila Vasilievna repeated her question. I scratched my nose, gathered up my thoughts, and answered: "I came to you for the impossible."

"Well, come in," she replied, intrigued by my answer.

Liudmila Vasilievna offered me a chair in front of her luxurious desk, which really was quite similar to the one in my imagination in the middle of the rye field. Many of the same objects from the imaginary desk were also present on the real one, with some slight differences. Most interesting was a large, round clock with a barometer on its opposite face. A wide window sill—the kind you find in old buildings—was covered with well-tended flower pots. A three-channel radio and electric kettle stood in a corner, and bunches of herbs were drying over the radiator.

"So what do you have for me?" asked Liudmila Groznaya.

"Well, as I said, I came for the impossible. The certificate I need usually takes at least two weeks to be processed, but I need it right away," I handed her the folder with my paperwork.

She carefully looked through my documents and said: "Would you like some tea?"

Confused by her offer, I refused.

"Then I'll turn on some music for you."

As it turned out, there was no music playing that day between two and three o'clock; evidently, the disk jockey was at lunch. "I'm sorry, but there's no music. Please wait here," Liudmila Vasilievna said, and she left the room.

I looked around and noticed two fishing poles in the corner. While I was trying to figure out who they might belong to, Liudmila Vasilievna returned with the certificate, opened a drawer, and took out a stamp. She stamped the certificate twice, signed it, and, pulling out a thick record book, wrote something in it. Then she showed me a check on the page and politely requested my signature. I signed it mechanically, and Liudmila Vasilievna gave me back the documents with a smile: "You see, nothing is impossible!"

This was followed by a minute or two of awkward silence. I couldn't think of anything to say, as the situation was utterly surreal. She finally broke the silence by talking about the flowers on the window sill. She was especially proud of a rare plant with hairy leaves and numerous tiny, white flowers. This plant had been brought to her from somewhere far away, and it took a long time to recover. Liudmila Vasilievna told me how she had fertilized it, even talked to it, and in the end it began to grow.

Finally I gathered my wits to thank her: "You can't imagine what a great help you've been. You're an amazing person! I'm really beginning to believe that nothing is impossible."

Liudmila Vasilievna was smiling happily. She agreed with me completely. I was already moving to the door, when I remembered: "Oh, I've forgotten to pay you."

"Oh, no! What are you saying?" she said, waving her arms in protest.

"I mean the fee for the document."

"Aw, yes!" she exclaimed, clapping her hands in surprise. "I completely forgot."

I paid her and left. I don't even remember descending the stairs to the street.

My friend, Alla, didn't believe my story about Liudmila Groznaya. Alla also had tried to submit documents to that department. She thought that I made the whole story up, because she was sure that documents are processed only after you submit your payment receipt. I could only smile mysteriously.

I had been so busy with the apartment, that I totally forgot about the second part of my wish—the cottage in the country. I was reminded of this when I received a phone call from a friend who owned a cottage in the village Malakhovka. "Today my husband gave a ride to a man who turned out to be our neighbor. He owns a section of a house here in Malakhovka, and wants to sell it. He needs the money right away, so he won't be asking much. Do you think you might be interested?"

I was dumbstruck. I had hardly recovered from the affair of the apartment, when the cottage suddenly appeared. I arranged a meeting and the next day went to view the house. It turned out there was a small plot of land attached to it as well. It was located just a hundred meters from the station near a pond, and gas and telephone service were already hooked up. I was actually glad to have only a section of the house, so that my neighbors could keep an eye on things while I was away. After speaking with the owner, I was both happy and sad at the same time. The owner was asking $6000, normally the price of an undeveloped lot in this district, but I managed to bargain him down to $4500. The problem was I had only $1500! I hoped that fortune would smile on me and the money would somehow appear.

That evening a friend came over to visit. For hours we discussed how I might make improvements on the land and in the cottage. So he was somewhat surprised when he found out that I was making all these plans before I even had the money to buy it. At that moment another friend, Semyon, called me on the phone. I hadn't seen him for nearly six months. As I picked up the phone, he caught the end of my conversation about not having enough money, and asked me how much I needed. Forty minutes later Semyon had arrived, dressed in a velvet suit, with French brandy and a bag of fruit. We celebrated the purchase of my cottage with music and candlelight. There were $3000 on the table, which Semyon had lent me interest free for an unlimited period of time.

That's how I got my apartment and a cottage.

ON THE BENEFITS OF BORSCHT

A woman named Natasha used to bring her six-year-old son to me for massage. One day she arrived in a very confused, emotional state. Her strained, breaking voice and the tense features of her face revealed feelings of irritation and indignation. It turned out that these feelings were caused by a young man named Yuri, who was her tenant. Over time, Yuri had turned the apartment into part open house and part storeroom. Mountains of cardboard and wooden boxes were piled up everywhere, and suspicious characters were constantly hanging around. Moreover, a pile of unpaid long-distance telephone bills was growing rapidly. Finally, with much effort, Natasha managed to evict Yuri. However, besides the unpaid telephone bills, he also owed her a large sum of money in back rent.

"What a loser! Not only didn't he pay the rent, but he talked endlessly on the phone to people all over the Soviet Union," raged Natasha, boiling over with righteous indignation.

I tried to explain to her that every person is a magician and can alter the course of events for the better. When I suggested that she give thanks to this obstacle which had appeared in her life, Natasha protested vehemently: "Thank that little bastard? Never! I only see him standing around with his pinkie sticking up like some kind of aristocrat!"

When I told her more about the successes of various magicians, Natasha calmed down and began to discuss her situation with less anger. She pictured herself and Yuri sitting next to each other at a table covered with an exquisite cloth. On this table was a bowl of thick, steaming borscht exuding an alluring aroma. Golden pools of butter, encircling chunks of meat, potatoes, beets, cabbage and other ingredients, floated in the rich, burgundy-colored broth. Yuri was wearing a lacey, white bib, and Natasha was carefully feeding him from the bowl with a large spoon. The new name for Natasha became: *"I am the one who feeds borscht to Yuri."* She confirmed that the name was appropriate, even bragging that her borscht was, in fact, excellent.

I recommended that Natasha picture herself feeding Yuri borscht whenever she thought about him or had any contact with him. Natasha left in an exhilarated state of mind.

About a week later she turned up again and straightaway, while still in the doorway, joyfully informed me that Yuri had paid off his debt completely, much to the surprise of her relatives and friends. The most interesting outcome, though, was that Yuri had begun calling Natasha frequently, showering her with flattery and compliments. He amused her with jokes and even dropped unequivocal hints that he had an interest in her, which had never happened before. While telling me all this, Natasha indifferently shrugged her shoulders and, with a disdainful expression on her face, declared: "All of this, of course, means nothing to me." However, in my opinion, that was just her little game, and I surmised that Natasha had most likely listened with pleasure to Yuri's "sweet serenades." This was confirmed immediately when her face lit up with a satisfied smile as she blurted out: "It looks like I fed him too much borscht!"

TO THE VICTIMS OF
FINANCIAL PYRAMIDS

This story took place in 1994, the year when the Russian people were consumed by "gold fever." Every street corner in Moscow was peppered with advertisements, in which various commercial banks, financial institutions, and joint stock companies promised fabulous returns on investments. The advertising superstars—Rita and Lyonia Golubkov—were ever-present on television, exhorting you to join the treasure hunt. Their line was simple and based on that age-old seducer—to accumulate huge sums of money for nothing. They played on a belief in miracles, which the Russian people are so prone to.

Everywhere were long lines of fervent gamblers, who were prepared to stand for days in front of the alluring doors which warmed their hearts with hope, where a "large bale of fresh hay" awaited them (cf. the tales about Nasrudin). They rushed to throw away the money burning holes in their pockets, willingly allowing themselves to be saddled by yet another donkey herder, who in turn was a donkey himself, obsessed by those bits of paper with presidential portraits on them.

I, too, caught this "gold fever," especially after one of my friends from Podolsk told me how, after investing money in Vlastilina several times over, he was able to buy a one-room apartment and a Zhiguli car. All that remained to do was decide which institution to give my money to. After some reflection, I selected the joint stock company Hermes-Finance. This company was a subsidiary of the firm Hermes, which now and then turned up in the media and therefore seemed respectable. In comparison with other investment companies, Hermes-Finance offered a smaller interest rate, but this very fact seemed in some way to make it more trustworthy. Besides that, the investment was insured, although Hermes itself was the insuring entity. Throwing caution to the wind, I jumped onto the bandwagon.

It was the middle of May. The sun was shining in a clear, blue sky. The chestnut trees were in bloom, thrusting their red and white pyramid-shaped flowers up into the sky.

Everything pointed to a favorable outcome. Public transport was running on time; there were no lines or delays along the way; the entryway into the building wasn't crowded. Inside everything appeared orderly and proper—a large, bright office with tables decorated with arranged flowers. Nice, well-mannered women in business suits politely familiarized customers with the necessary information and recorded deposits. Nothing portended any complications. I deposited my money for the minimum period of three months, counting on 50% interest.

Over the summer, however, clouds began gathering over such investment funds for the common people. The huge financial bubble of MMM, a gigantic investment firm, suddenly burst. The Podolsk company Vlastilina stopped paying out deposits, the Bank of Tibet collapsed, and so on. But Hermes-Finance was still afloat, and at the end of August I went to collect my dividends.

In light of recent events, I was wavering over what I should do. Take out all of my money? Or only take out my initial investment, leaving the interest in for another three months. The temptation of snatching up yet another "free bale of hay" was too great to resist—I decided to play the game again. As they say: "A faint heart never won a fair lady!" The clerk registering my new investment betrayed a slight anxiety and nervousness in her attitude, but even this didn't stop me—the fish was already caught in the net. Besides, I had recovered my original investment and was only risking the "free" money.

That autumn "Black Tuesday" came crashing down, and within days the ruble had lost two thirds of its value. I gave thanks to Vanya, but the situation was already out of control. The time came "to gather the stones together." On the appointed day, I went to the now familiar office of Hermes-Finance.

A peevish crowd had gathered outside the armor-plated door of the building. It was immediately clear that, using the ruble's default as an excuse, payout of deposits had almost come to a standstill. Money was being given only to those who were supposed to have received their payment on the second or third day after "Black Tuesday," and even then only small sums were being paid out. The door opened a bit and from it emerged a somewhat embarrassed but fortunate man who had managed to get back his hard-earned cash with interest. The enraged investors pressed forward, trying to force their way through the gap in the door until a formally-dressed officer appeared, calling the people to order. He tried to explain the situation but met only anger and indignation, so he quickly retreated, slamming the door behind him.

A rather scruffy-looking old man with a red face explained to me that, in order to have any hope of getting my money, I had to somehow get inside to have my contract stamped. When the door finally cracked open again, I managed to push my way in. An irritated secretary slapped a ludicrous stamp on my contract stating: "At the present time there is no money available, and the process of paying out funds has slowed. Please call later for more information." I recalled Pushkin's tale "The Fisherman and the Fish" with its instructive moral.*

When I emerged back on the street, breathing in the icy-fresh air, I finally was able to catch my breath. It was dark and snow was falling. The city all around was living its own life, and an endless stream of cars flowed along the ring road Sadovoye Koltso. Breathing in the light frost sobered me up.

I defocused my eyes, and the Moscow lights were transformed in my imagination into colorful fireworks, glittering tinsel, and Christmas garlands. A tall, bushy Christmas tree, turquoise in color, was decorated with tropical fruits and flowers, and crowned with an enamel chamber pot. Grandfather Frost was sitting on top wearing a long, white Bedouin robe. Exotic animals danced merrily around the tree.

After that, instead of regretting my lost profit, I invoked the picture of the Christmas tree with the animals dancing around it. Time passed, and my telephone calls to Hermes-Finance were getting me nowhere. Deposits were not being returned, and nobody was answering the phone. Remembering that magicians do not press issues to proceed faster than they should, I stopped trying to force my way through the locked doors. Occasionally, the common world view took control of me. How could I get my lost money back? But I continued dancing around the Christmas tree.

At times I felt like changing my imaginary movie—to remove some aspect, to add more detail, to introduce new characters. For example, the mischievous Old Lady Shapoklyak could emerge from behind the Christmas tree dressed as Snow White. She could climb up onto a stool and sing a

* In this famous tale, the fisherman's wife keeps asking the magical fish for more and more favors. She eventually attains royal status, and when even this is not enough to satisfy her, the fish transforms her back into her original condition as a poor, old fisherman's wife sitting in front of a cracked washtub. [trans]

popular Russian song in an operatic voice: "We are mowing down the magic grassy grasses."

As so often happens with magicians, the final result far exceeded all expectations. After the New Year, my wife received several lump sums of money which were a complete surprise to her. The total amount of this "reward" was far more than the money lost in the ruins of the financial pyramid.

TALE OF THE LITTLE BUDDHA

Dedicated to all who have lost hope.

This chapter is about a man who discovered amazing magical powers within himself, and thus was able to untangle the complex knot of inner contradictions underlying his life's problems. The narrative illustrates how you can find a way out of despair and make a new start in this drama we call life.

This story in no way attempts to give all the details of the affair, but what we have included here shows a real life case of the familiar story of the ugly duckling. Hats off, my friends! The show is about to begin...

A PROPHETIC DREAM

One morning, I received a phone call from Sasha. I had known him for about three years as a sociable and fun-loving fellow, so I was greatly surprised to hear that for most of his life he had been tormented by constant headaches. Recently, the pain had increased, and Sasha, having heard of our system of practical magic, was hoping I could help him.

It was the end of August, and the following day I was leaving for the Crimea. Time was short, but for now I promised to magnetize* some water for him, and then we could work more intensively together when I returned to Moscow. The

following day I brought him a bottle of magnetized water.
Sasha's condition had definitely declined. I had never seen
him in such a miserable state, but the healing water and our
brief conversation seemed to cheer him up.

When I returned from the Crimea two weeks later, I became absorbed in the everyday hustle and bustle of life and
completely forgot about Sasha. However, for about a week I
was haunted by a vague feeling of dissatisfaction, as if I had
overlooked something. Then one night I had a dream.

It took place on a huge iceberg. A narrow footpath wound
along the very top, and beyond loomed a bottomless abyss. In
my dream I was an unknown actor from a small town, surrounded by famous theater and movie stars. A comedy was
being performed, and the stars—Gundareva, Tabakov, Dzhi-
garkhanian, Kramarov—played their roles joyously and with
ease. There was no script, just free improvisation. The action
proceeded in most unexpected ways, and the sets were constantly changing. I, too, had a humorous part to play, but my
acting was neither natural nor brilliant.

I felt very constrained. I kept stumbling on my words,
and my lines were awkward and out of place. I couldn't relax
with that gaping abyss yawning below me. Every once in a
while, I would look down into the emptiness and a shudder
would pass down my spine. The actors exchanged meaningful
glances each time I made another blunder.

The same thought kept passing through my mind: "I wish
it would just be over."

Suddenly, without warning, the play abruptly ended, and
the actors gathered together in a tight circle, pronouncing

---

* For more details about "magnetizing" water, cf. the story
"Goldilocks."

their merciless verdict: "You played your role horribly; you were not funny at all."

A heavy silence fell over the group. Then the famous actress, Gundareva, stepped forward: "Maybe we should give him another chance."

Buldakov, as always a cigar between his lips, growled: "What on earth are you talking about?"

The rest of them shrugged their shoulders and, after brief consideration, agreed.

Upon awakening, the memory of the dream was so clear, so vivid, that in comparison everyday reality seemed like a pale imitation of life. As I left my apartment, I tried hard to remember the details of the dream. Heading downtown, I noticed three men at the end of the train platform pouring out a bottle of Stolichnaya vodka into paper cups. This instantly reminded me of a forgotten fragment of my dream.

The stage of ice had transformed into an auditorium with heavy, burgundy-colored curtains. In the middle was a long table covered with various delicacies, around which sat the participants in the previous performance. The famous Russian actor, Andrey Mironov, in the role of Ostap Bender, rose up from the table, slugged down a mouthful of vodka straight from a flask, flung his white scarf over his shoulder, pulled down his cap, and proclaimed: "The trial continues, ladies and gentlemen of the jury!"

The circle of events had been completed: the guys with the Stolichnaya; the great con man, Ostap Bender with a flask of vodka; the bottle of magnetized water—Sasha! The dream somehow related to him. This was where the vague feeling of dissatisfaction had come from. I immediately gave thanks to Vanya for warning me that I might always forget to keep my promises to friends, and I sent him a gift in the form of a windmill with sails made from peacock feathers.

I finally managed to get through to Sasha's wife, Irina, very late that night. Her voice breaking, she told me: "Sasha is much worse. The pain is not getting any better; it has become unbearable. Just yesterday I took him to the hospital."

Not far from my home is a soccer field. As I passed it the next day, one of the boys was charging for the goal. I thought to myself: "If he misses, then Sasha can be saved. But if he scores a goal, everything is lost." The ball went straight through the goalposts. Could nothing really be done? The memories of my dream again flooded my mind. They had said: "Should we give him another chance?" It suddenly struck me that the dream was about Sasha!

I remembered Sasha back when we had worked together. His face was always lit up with a smile, and he got along well with everyone. I never once saw him angry or annoyed, even when he was worn down by his headaches. What inner strength he had shown! Irina told me later that for a long time after their marriage even she didn't know that he was in severe pain. She only began to suspect when she noticed that he was secretly taking pills. Could it be that such a person would be unable to overcome his illness? Get thee away, doubts! "The trial continues, ladies and gentlemen of the jury."

A TRIP TO VENICE

I arranged with Irina to visit Sasha in the hospital. She worked there as a doctor and offered to let us use her office. She explained to me his complete diagnosis. He had enough ailments for the entire hospital! My mind was boggled by the numerous erudite medical terms, and I finally stopped even listening. As a professional doctor, Irina understood that even one from this "bouquet" of ailments was enough to send someone into the next world—for example, arachnoiditis, inflammation of the brain tissue, which conventional medicine considers to be incurable.

However, Irina had not lost hope. She lived with Sasha in a suburb of Moscow called Nekrasovka, where the hospital also was located. Irina gave me a temporary pass, and at the appointed time I arrived at the hospital. Sasha looked terrible. His face was pale, waxen. He had the vacant gaze of a man with one foot already in the grave. He had lost his coordination and rocked jerkily from side to side.

Sasha, who was over forty, told me that he had suffered from these headaches since childhood. Nothing really had helped him—neither strong painkillers, nor repeated hospital treatments. Sasha had begun trying various spiritual practices—Dynamic Meditation, Raja Yoga, Reiki, the system of Porfiry Ivanov.* None of these was particularly effective, and

* This treatment includes bathing in ice-cold water twice a day and a total fast for forty hours per week. [trans]

his condition gradually became worse. It reached the point that he would lie flat on his back for several days only half aware of his surroundings. He suffered from vomiting, had memory blackouts, and sometimes even lost all sense of time and space. The periods between such bouts eventually decreased to only one or two hours a day. Sasha was taking two packets of pills each day, causing his digestive and immune systems to fall completely out of balance.

During our conversation, Sasha was as usual experiencing a severe headache. He was familiar with the magical world view, so it wasn't necessary to explain to him the idea of giving thanks. Sasha began by thanking his ailments and fears for warning him that they could push him straight into the grave. I suggested that Sasha conceive a new image of himself.

He sat back comfortably, closed his eyes, and saw an ancient well surrounded by sand. A thin trickle of water dribbled out of the well, which gradually grew into a steady stream. Soon the water had spread out everywhere, forming a smooth, glassy surface. Suddenly, delicate buildings, arched bridges, towers, roofs of houses, canals, and flights of stairs began emerging out of the water. Gondolas with elegantly dressed passengers were leisurely gliding along the canals. The setting sun tinted the clouds, buildings, and surface of the water with pink and gold tones. Sasha was inside an amazing picture. He was crossing Venice on a gondola.

To his surprise, Sasha noticed that his headache had disappeared. For the first time ever, he had managed to cope without pills or sedation. He was as happy as a child. While he was enjoying his triumph, I stood up and walked over to the window to stretch my legs. It had been an overcast, rainy day, but now the skies were clearing in the west, and the sun, hanging over the edge of the forest, gilded the veil of clouds, exactly as in his Venetian vision. Nature was confirming the quality of our work together! His new name was ready: *"I am the one who glides along Venetian canals."* For two days his headaches did not return. The newly-created gondolier proclaimed it a colossal achievement. This successful experience was enough to restore his faith in himself, and to convince him that "magic works!"

From that day on, he often set out for Venice, especially at the first signs of a headache. The spells without pain became longer; the process of renewal had begun.

THE SHARP-TOOTHED PIKE

Sasha admitted that one of the main obstacles preventing him from leading a harmonious life was the fear of death—fear of the abyss, at the edge of which he now found himself. In principle, Sasha was resigned to the idea that the fall is inevitable. He told me that, not long before the beginning of our work together, he had prepared himself to die, devising an efficient and dramatic departure from this life. More than once he had imagined how he would give all his friends his most cherished possessions, how, shedding a few manly tears, he would say goodbye to his wife, and then set off alone into the dark forest to die.

However, the specter of that bony old woman with a scythe was extremely frightening to him. Also, the fear of exhausting fits of pain filled him with dread. Whenever his pain abated somewhat, the fear of the next wave rose up again. We had to delve into this issue as soon as possible. Sasha tried to remember when he had experienced fear for the first time. The root event was uncovered almost at once.

When he was five years old, Sasha was on vacation in the country. One day, as he was returning home from the river, he saw a group of village boys sitting around bored. The eldest of them decided to tease little Sasha, and he unexpectedly pulled out a huge, half-dead pike. Opening its jaws wide, he jerked it toward Sasha's face. The fish was fluttering its gills and beating its tail. It is impossible to describe the effect this had on Sasha. The grown-ups who ran over to help him were hardly able to calm him down.

Sasha required a new name. He could not really offer thanks to the boys, since he did not know them at all. This meant that he had to recreate the root episode. Sasha settled on the following variation: when he noticed that the boys were bored, he went up to them and pulled a penknife out of his pocket. The boys' eyes brightened with interest, and Sasha's offer to play a game with the knife was gladly accepted. Time flew by, and when it was time for Sasha to go home, the eldest boy offered him the pike in exchange for his knife. Sasha was barely able to carry the large fish home. That was it! There was no fear, and Sasha received his new name: *"I am the one who suggests to the boys that we play a game with my penknife."*

After recreating the root episode, he felt a great relief, and his current fears seemed groundless. After that, whenever fear swept over him, Sasha repeated his new name, and his courage returned. At our next meeting, he showed me a support signal he had purchased—a notepad with a spotted, green pike on the cover. And I received further confirmation while writing this story: my wife was watching a movie called *Peculiarities of the National Hunt*. I glanced up at the screen and saw the drunken forester, Kuzmich, pulling a large pike out of the water.

BUDDHA IN A TUXEDO

Some time later Sasha was released from the hospital. Due to his rich imagination, he proved to be a gifted magician, and during one of our meetings, he told me the following story:

For as long as I can remember, I was never able to get along with my mother. We no longer lived together, but it was still very difficult. Telephone conversations with her were sheer punishment. She was always trying to tell me what to do—how to live, how to walk, how to eat, how to treat my wife. She would say, "You have turned into a complete fool. You are always doing things for your family, but they hardly even notice it (Sasha and Irina share their apartment with her daughter and son-in-law). Your wife is horrible—she never sews buttons on your clothes or cooks borscht for you." She constantly rebuked me for not looking after her or helping her at home. But whenever I tried to do something for her, she would tell me that whatever I did was wrong. A quiet, calm conversation inevitably grew into an argument, which always ended up with one hanging up on the other. It reached the point that, whenever I heard my mother's voice on the phone, my blood would boil over.

In order to give my mother tranquility, I imagined this internal movie: two concrete walls loudly crashing into each another. On impact they crumbled into dust. When the cloud of dust settled, I envisioned the Buddha soaring through the air above a forest glade. He was in his usual lotus position with a blissful smile, and a radiant aura shimmered around him.

However, it wasn't the usual Buddha you think of. This Buddha was dressed in an immaculate tuxedo with a bow tie and patent leather boots, and from his lips protruded a cigar. I gave myself the name: *"I am the Buddha who soars in a tuxedo."* Now, whenever I talk to my mother, I imagine myself in this form. I didn't have to wait long for results. After our next telephone conversation, I felt fully relaxed. We talked about everyday matters and said goodbye happily to each other. Since then our relationship has improved tremendously.

THE EMBROIDERED ELEPHANT

One by one the difficult psychological issues which Sasha had suffered from throughout his life were uncovered. I was constantly surprised when comparing the joyful and talkative Sasha, as I remembered him in the beginning of our friendship, with his current state—miserable and with low self-esteem. Gradually, I began to understand how this hero of our epic had managed to wind up in such straits.

The problem was that he was holding his issues and inner contradictions inside, over time stuffing them deeper and deeper. Unable to free himself, he was literally being torn to pieces, both his psychic body and his physical body, and any attempt to further suppress them had just the opposite effect— the samovar boiled over even more. It became a vicious circle. Sasha found a way out only when he *stopped struggling* against his ailments and fears, and instead began *thanking* them.

The next phase of our work addressed an issue faced by many people. It seemed to Sasha that no one needed him; he felt abandoned by everyone. This feeling of loneliness tormented Sasha, giving him no peace, and contributed to his loss of self-esteem. He always thought that he was doing something wrong, although he constantly tried to please everyone around him. He wasn't leading his own life, but rather the life which he thought others wanted him to lead. He was fully dependent on the opinions of others.

For example, Sasha had been involved in various schools of spiritual and personal development, some of which required a vegetarian diet. But Sasha loved meat, and at home he wolfed it down with gusto. But when he ate meals at meetings where there was no meat, he felt extremely awkward in front of others. Sasha told everyone that he didn't eat meat and suffered because, in reality, this was not true, and he craved meat very much. He was terribly worried that these people would find out that he "was defiling himself with impure food."

At one time the authors of this book were orthodox yogis and also refused to eat meat. We managed to convince ourselves of the superiority of a vegetarian diet, and our desire for meat completely disappeared. When we began practicing magic, however, we realized that we had accepted a world view which prohibited meat, automatically, as the "gospel truth." If you understand that any world view is an illusion, then you have the *freedom to choose which world view* to play in at any given moment. Obviously, it is better to choose a world view which gives more latitude than one which is restrictive. As before, we still prefer a vegetarian diet, but would not refuse a savory barbecue while picnicking in the country; we would enjoy it without the least bit of regret.

Sasha wanted to overcome his lack of confidence with strength, so he took up the Ivanov system. He practiced it very seriously, to the point that he was able to walk without hat or gloves during the fiercest winter frosts. He wore only a light Italian coat, T-shirt, jeans, and sandals without socks. Sasha managed to penetrate deeper into this world view than into the prohibition against meat, and his feet did not freeze.

Sasha has a rather unusual, even comical external appearance. He is short and stocky, with a few wisps of hair on his large, bald head and a bushy, gray beard. His unnaturally huge eyes, enlarged even more by the thick lenses of his glasses, and good-natured expression complete the portrait. He also has thick, crooked fingers which resemble the claws of a crab.

One magician gave him the nickname "the hobgoblin," and another "the alien."

When this lightly-dressed hobgoblin in sandals walked onto the train or subway in wintertime, he was tormented by insecurity. "What do people think of me?" he wondered. It appeared that everyone was glancing sidelong at him and whispering behind his back. It would seem strange that, having achieved very impressive results—such as walking barefoot in the snow—he was constantly tormented by lack of self-esteem and feelings of worthlessness.

Many esoteric schools preach an ascetic attitude toward material comforts. Through spiritual practice, their followers cultivate a contempt for the "fallen world" (yet another world view). Ideally, a seeker of enlightenment must be a ragged and hungry beggar. The authors are only too familiar with this "ancient tradition." Sasha was also hooked on it. He relied on the opinions of others, including the "great" masters and teachers, not allowing himself to buy the things he wanted—for instance, a cassette recorder and television. It wasn't that he didn't want these things, but that "he mustn't!" What's more, Sasha had been taught in one of the esoteric schools that all his illnesses, hardships, and the everyday mess of his life were, in fact, signs of his high level of achievement, a kind of super mutation foreshadowing his coming ascension!

Sasha had to sort out his internal contradictions. Turning to his personal story, we began to look for the root episode. He quickly recalled three successive episodes, in which he experienced strong feelings of alienation and lack of self-esteem.

In one, he was nine or ten years old. His mother had recently given birth to twins—a little brother and sister—and Sasha always had to baby sit them. His friends were outside running around, playing ball, riding their bikes, but he had to sit home with the twins. He was bitter and of-fended by this.

An earlier episode happened when Sasha was seven. At that time, he was living at a boarding school in the country. There was a tight-knit group of children there who bullied and teased him for his physical problems. Feeling unwanted by anyone, he ran off into the forest. Here it was—the original script for his beautiful death by disappearing into a deep, dark forest.

Finally, the root episode was revealed. Sasha was three or four years old. He recalled the communal barracks they lived in with a dim lamp in the corridor. There was one kitchen for ten families with a rickety table and wooden stools—as in the song by Vysotsky: "Only one toilet for thirty-eight rooms." Sasha had gotten into trouble, and his mother rudely pushed him, saying: "Go away, I don't want you here. You're a bad boy!" This was actually a way of "renaming" him, only the op-posite. Sasha went into hysterics. His own mother didn't want him! He ran up to her, but again she pushed him away. "I'm not your mother!" she yelled at him. Sasha was consumed with a sense of overwhelming fear. The world became unbearable to him. He leaned over a stool and started blubbering. He could still remember the nail heads there pounded into the unpainted stool.

This time Sasha thanked his mother for warning him that he could continue to weep crocodile tears of grief over his loneliness for the rest of his life. In order to return to his mother (and thus to himself) the emotional balance and self-esteem which they both lacked, Sasha began searching for some relevant positive memory. At last he found it, and what a memory it was!

His mother had taught him how to embroider. She gave him wooden frames and materials—pieces of thick, white canvas and embroidery thread. Sasha enjoyed this pastime. He copied a picture onto the cloth using carbon paper and began to embroider with cross and satin stitches. His mother wondered what he was so diligently working on, but Sasha kept his work a secret. It took him about two months to complete, but at last the embroidery was done—a blue and yellow elephant with a burgundy-colored flower. At last the long-awaited moment came. When his mother opened the door and entered his room, Sasha ran up to her and exclaimed: "Happy Mother's Day, mommy!" Then he triumphantly pulled out the embroidery from behind his back. His mother wept with joy, stroking his hair lovingly.

What a moment! I sprang up from the couch like an excited hunter who has tracked down some rare animal. The name was ready: *"I am the one who embroiders mommy an elephant."* At that moment, it was hard to even recognize Sasha; the man sitting in front of me was a completely changed person. In an attempt to express the state of inner freedom which overwhelmed him, he offered this metaphor: "It was like I had been locked up for an eternity, and suddenly my prison door was thrown wide open before me." Right after Sasha spoke these words, a strong gust of wind blew open the window, and a flow of fresh air rushed into the room! Utterly enchanted, we gazed at the open window in absolute silence.

Gradually, Sasha's confidence grew stronger. With each small victory, it became easier for him. And the easier it became, the more deeply Sasha discovered the freedom within him. He started being himself more often, doing what he wanted to do. Now Sasha scarfs down meat at meetings without a second thought. During the winter he freely walks around in his sandals. "Looking closer, I see that nobody is really paying any attention to me. There wasn't actually any problem at all. It was just my own fantasies, my internal dialogue."

Sasha learned to attach less significance to various dogmas. He started earning more money and bought himself an imported cassette recorder, stereo system, television, and VCR. More than a year has passed since that day when Sasha began to "embroider the elephant" and, looking at him now, we can say that he has become much more liberated in how he lives his life. However, it is not quite yet time to crown him with the wreath of victory—sometimes the old tape loop starts playing through again.

In speaking about his latest success, Sasha made this comparison: "Imagine that your leg was broken and in a cast for a long time. When the cast is finally removed, you can feel your leg, now able to move, begin to return to life, to 'breathe' again." Whenever Sasha relied more on himself, all his pains and ailments would simply vanish.

Boat in a storm

Sasha felt significantly stronger physically, his coordination improved, and he no longer shook like a reed blowing in the wind. His face radiated health, his stomach stopped hurting, his heartburn disappeared, his digestion improved, and his constipation was alleviated. He even began to look younger. Irina remarked happily that he had become more like the former Sasha—agile and upbeat.

His confidence in his own power was growing—in his words, he "found his inner core." Previously, he used to say that he could not do without a spiritual shepherd to guide him. However, after discovering magic Sasha began to realize more and more that the need for a teacher is actually an admission of one's own lack of self-confidence. It is a convenient way to lay responsibility onto the shoulders of the one who leads, whose flock the lost sheep has joined.

Not long ago, Sasha shared with me this allegory:

My life reminds me of sailing in a boat. I used to always be afraid that I would find myself alone in my tiny vessel in the vast ocean and end up drowning. I thought that it would be safer to join a fleet, where there are many boats including huge cruisers which could tow me along behind them, and with a flagship which would know the true course. But when a storm rose up, my frail skiff was suddenly alone again in the turbulent sea. My boat would become so swamped with water that I constantly had to bail it out to survive. Figuring that I must have chosen the wrong fleet, I joined another.

The next fleet had a courageous captain—a true sea dog. He spoke so eloquently, promising to lead us to new lands, rich and vast, like in fairytales. But another storm came, and again I found myself alone. This time my boat was filled even more with water.

The leader of the next fleet was a stern admiral. He put delinquents in chains in the galley. The sailors trembled before him and respected him for this. But again the storm came, and I floundered. This time the water rose up to the very top of my boat.

For years I wandered from one flotilla to another but could only just manage to stay afloat.

Then I noticed how the wind filled out my baggy boxer underwear. "Maybe I should try to use it as a sail," I thought. As soon as I fixed my underwear onto the mast, my boat rushed forward. It turned out to be quite easy to navigate. The main thing was to catch a good wind, and then everything fell into place.

Soon I felt like a real "old salt." My sailboat dashed along so quickly that the water which had splashed in slopped overboard on its own. I learned to discern the subtle signs of imminent foul weather, and to change course to evade the storm. I realized that in time even my boxer underwear would no longer be needed. I will simply steer into a warm current, and my boat will be carried along with it. Then, if my vessel deviates from the rushing stream, I'll only have to make a slight adjustment of the rudder, and soon I'll again be speeding forward.

A CLOUD OF WHITE
APPLE BLOSSOMS*

Let's return to the time when our hero started "soaring in a tuxedo." Sasha had improved his relationship with his mother, but he wanted to take his success further. The magic scent of freedom was intoxicating to him. It was time to take up another hard nut to crack—his wife. Here is a typical scene in their family life from that time.

Sasha is looking forward to his wife coming home from work. He is happy when she arrives, but Irina is in a foul mood. "My boss didn't pay me again! They keep piling all the work on me, and then they complain about what I do. What's more, I have nothing to wear any more—no boots, no winter coat, nothing! And then my husband is always sick, and my daughter is unemployed; in fact, her whole life is a mess!"

Sasha frowns. His mood has been ruined; his happiness has vanished. A splitting headache starts coming on. In the end, no one wins—Irina is suffering, Sasha is flat on his back, and her daughter, Masha, runs away, slamming the door behind her.

Here is another example: The family is experiencing financial difficulties, but this time it is Sasha's harsh words which cause the quarrel. He rebukes Masha for sitting around all day not working while they have to feed her. Then Irina bursts

* A line from a popular Russian song. [trans]

144

into a rage: "So my daughter is in your way! You're forgetting that I'm supporting you! I'm taking care of you! You don't even care anymore; you don't understand! You used to love me, but now you hardly even notice me!"

Sasha gave thanks to Irina for warning him that their family life could turn into a complete nightmare. I suggested to Sasha that he look for the *ray of light*—some event which encapsulates the mutual love and understanding which brought them together. Sasha found the perfect episode.

In the beginning of our relationship, we were a unified whole. We always knew what the other was feeling. One evening I visited Irina, and we went out onto her balcony. It was spring, and everything around was bursting with life. The air was still and the birds were singing. A sublime fragrance wafted up from the apple trees blossoming below. We were admiring the rising full moon, the stars. We hugged each other, gazing deep into each other's eyes. Together we experienced such bliss, such understanding and love, which I had never felt anywhere before. Then we kissed…

Sasha told me how, after their next date, Irina had flown home on wings of love. Her happiness was so great that it took her breath away. At home, she talked the whole night to her daughter about Sasha, saying that at last she had met her soul mate.

Sasha gave Irina a new name: *"I am the one who is kissing on the balcony"* and *"I am the one who flies home on wings of love after meeting my soul mate."* He became more watchful, and when misunderstandings arose, he renamed Irina with one of her new names. And whenever he felt that his wife might come home in a bad mood, he would do this in advance. Sometimes he forgot, and then he had to rename her in the heat of an argument when, lashing out at him with harsh words, Irina would rush off to the kitchen. He didn't allow himself to become upset, as would have happened before, but instead repeated her new names. Consequently, after some fifteen or twenty minutes, she would return calmed down, as if nothing had happened. She would walk up to Sasha and explain: "I didn't mean it, Sasha. You know how sometimes I just get into a bad mood." Irina was changing before his eyes.

Sasha was amazed at how quickly his renaming of her was working, how it was transforming his wife. He would "kiss on the balcony" and "fly on wings of love" whenever circumstances required it. However, the need to do this became less and less frequent. Now Sasha calmly and confidently fine-tunes his relationship with his wife. It is interesting to note that he has changed as well, and now gives her fewer reasons for discord.

HOW SASHA BEFRIENDED PETYA

After sorting out his relationship with Irina, Sasha turned his attention to his son-in-law, Petya. He had always been extremely uncomfortable in his presence. Their relationship reminded him of a battlefield—constant quarrelling, tension, and dividing up possessions and territory. Days would pass without any word passing between them. Nor did Petya get along with his mother-in-law, and this affected Sasha, too. Sasha's son-in-law completely ignored his health problems, and when Sasha wasn't feeling well, Petya would turn up his music full blast.

Petya was a terribly destructive person. Everything he owned—especially his television set and car—regularly broke down. Whatever he touched would break, burn out, or fall apart. Once his bed suddenly just collapsed under him.

Sasha made up his mind to rename his son-in-law by remembering a good deed he had done for him. Once, when Petya had purchased a car, he was in desperate need of tools. Sasha often helped him out. It was easy to choose his name: *"I am the one who gives Petya a wrench."* After this, a cease fire seemed to settle on the "front" between them, but the tension persisted. Once Petya's Samsung television suddenly exploded with a loud bang, strewing the floor with bits of glass. Sasha called me, and I gave him the mantra DURRBINTK. The breakdowns stopped happening.

Whenever Sasha felt that communication with Petya was becoming tense, he started repeating the mantra, and suddenly he saw before him a completely different man. In Sasha's figurative way of expressing things, it was as if Petya had received a huge cash bonus.

Once Sasha met his son-in-law on the way home from work. Petya was sullen and uncommunicative. He didn't even greet Sasha. They went into the apartment together, but Sasha immediately left to take the dog out for a walk. During this walk, Sasha diligently sang DURRBINTK. When he returned home, he was pleasantly surprised. Petya came into his room, a very rare occurrence, and said benevolently: "Sasha, you should watch this video. It's a fantasy film, and I know how you like fantasy." As for his music, he no longer plays it at all in the apartment. Furthermore, Petya is unremitting in his concern for Sasha's health. He constantly reminds Masha and Irina to be quiet, "because Sasha is tired today and needs rest."

HAULING IN THE POTATOES

One day during the summer, Irina brought home the sad news that her father's health had taken a turn for the worse. Lately, Boris Nikolaevich, who was in his 70's, could barely walk, and his medical tests deeply concerned the family. Irina's spirits had sunk completely, as she prepared for her father's death. Sighing grievously, she raced about the apartment, unable to calm herself, from time to time exclaiming in despair: "Where will we possibly get money for the funeral?"

Sasha sank deep into thought. Was there a time when he had done something to nourish his father-in-law's well-being? At last he remembered such an episode.

It was a warm, sunny day in early autumn. Harvest time was in full swing at Boris Nikolaevich's summerhouse. Just married, Sasha and Irina came to help. On the day they arrived, his father-in-law had planned to haul several large sacks of potatoes into the cellar, but after an argument with his wife, Xenia, he was too stressed and couldn't be bothered with the potatoes.

Sasha suggested to him: "Boris Nikolaevich! Take it easy; have a smoke and relax. I will haul in the potatoes." And so it happened. Sasha easily carried in all of the sacks, and, in the meantime, Boris Nikolaevich pulled himself together and went to make peace with Xenia. His wife also had cooled down, and they were able to talk it out.

That night Boris Nikolaevich confided in Xenia: "That Sasha is a good fellow! He really helped me out today. I didn't really expect him to care enough to pitch in. I'm really grateful to him." Next day Boris Nikolaevich had a burst of energy and continued the harvest with great enthusiasm.

This was a perfect episode to work with, and Sasha gave himself this new name: *"I am the one who hauls in bags of potatoes."* A few days later, Irina visited her father at his summerhouse and returned home in complete ecstasy. Boris Nikolaevich was feeling like he was in his twenties. In only a couple days, he had finished some repairs which he had expected to take two or three months. He re-shingled and stained a section of the roof, dug half his vegetable garden, fixed the fence, and repaired the car. Boris Nikolaevich used to tire out very quickly. He did everything grudgingly, at a snail's pace. He would work a little, and then sit back and rest. Now it was like he was on fire. He had changed, literally, right in front of their eyes. He was stronger, and looked as if he had just returned from a restful vacation.

Now Sasha was convinced that his father-in-law's ailments could be managed. Whenever he started feeling under the weather, Sasha would "haul in the potatoes." This summer Boris Nikolaevich again shocked his family—he re-shingled the rest of the roof! Admiring his achievement, he would say: "I never dreamed that I could do it. I thought I would come here and just sit around doing nothing. Where did all this energy come from? I've now re-shingled the entire house! You see, there's still life left in this old boy!"

DOWN WITH EXPLOITATION OF WORKERS!

On weekends Sasha used to work a second job as a security officer for the firm "Wings and Tails." On his first day at work, the director Yegorych, puffing up with importance, proclaimed: "We are doing you a great favor. You know how hard these times are with so much unemployment everywhere. I trust you will prove yourself worthy."

At the beginning of his work at the firm, Sasha was glad to offer his help and willingly performed extra duties. He never refused to work overtime. He did not suspect that he had fallen into the grip of shameless tyrants. However, over time his exploitation exceeded all bounds. The director made Sasha work during holidays without pay. Besides his duties as a security guard, Yegorych assigned him janitorial work; he had to load and unload equipment, assemble and dismantle bicycles, and perform various other tasks. The director would always remind him what a great favor it was for him to have a job at all.

Sasha thanked the director for warning him that he could end up a slave, laboring for free on Yegorych's "plantation." In order to rename himself, Sasha searched for a time when he had helped the director accomplish something he really needed done. Such an episode had taken place at the dawn of Sasha's patriotic service for the firm "Wings and Tails." At that time, the director was confronted with a difficult problem concerning financial relations with some other firms. Unable to find a solution, the boss had turned to Sasha for help.

Generally speaking, in Yegorych's opinion, Sasha "wasn't all there"—he listened to depressing music, read peculiar books, walked around in sandals during the winter, and always talked about some sort of weird spiritual teachings and practices. What exactly these teachings were, Yegorych had no idea, but, because he had no one else to turn to, he asked Sasha: "Could your teachings help me sort out this problem?" Sasha performed his magic that evening, and the issue was resolved.

The following day Yegorych came in very happy and thanked Sasha: "You have done me a great favor." If at that point Sasha, who "wasn't all there," had stopped offering to perform any additional services, his subsequent exploitation by the director would most likely have never become an issue.

Sasha renamed himself: *I am the one who does a great favor for Yegorych.* As soon as he started repeating this name, the director's attitude toward him changed dramatically. All the extra duties and overtime ceased. On top of that, Sasha also got a pay raise. Once Yegorych said to him in passing: "We will keep you here, not for the sake of God, but as *a little Buddha!*"

Since that time, Sasha has had only one occasion to recall the name invoking his "great favor." Yegorych was considering taking on an additional worker, a carpenter named Vasya who had worked there previously but had a weakness for drink. If he was hired, Sasha's hours would be cut, and he'd earn less money. So he kept his eyes open and again started doing his "great favor." In the end, Yegorych decided that it wasn't worth taking the risk, and that it was better to have the little Buddha than big Vasya.

EPILOGUE

Before the curtain descends on our story, we will allow Sasha a final word:

Over time my awareness of being a magician, of having inner knowledge has increased—more exactly, not so much knowledge as skill. It's like swimming. You might understand intellectually how to swim, and yet still not be able to do it. I felt that I really knew how to be a magician—not book knowledge, but rather an inner knowledge transmitted through everyday experience. It's one thing to read or hear about something, but quite another to *get 'er done*. It's as if I'm merging with the magician within me. It's difficult to describe in words. Sometimes during dancing you can feel a deep connection with your partner, an inner resonance between the two of you, and then you don't need to worry so much about doing the movements exactly right, or moving in perfect symmetry together. Everything happens of itself, and you become one with your partner.

We invite you, too, to dance with us, dear reader. The end of this tale has not yet been written. "The trial continues, ladies and gentlemen of the jury!"

MAGICAL CURES

The whole modern conception of the world is founded on the illusion that the so-called laws of nature are the
explanations of natural phenomena. Thus people today
stop at the laws of nature, treating them as something in-
violable, just as God and Fate were treated in past ages.
  Ludwig Wittgenstein—*Tractatus Logico-Philosophicus*

HEALING

Magical techniques are universal, and this is, without doubt,
their greatest attribute. If only one of these techniques is
learned well, you can apply it literally to any problem—you
can change the weather, improve your standard of living, or
whatever else you may desire. I wanted to cut my teeth on a
particularly difficult challenge and was given an opportunity
for this last March.

A psychic friend named Tolya was visiting me, and we were
talking leisurely over tea. Suddenly an idea struck me, and I
suggested to Tolya that we conduct an experiment to test the
power of magical dance on one of his patients. Tolya agreed
and immediately chose a female patient for the experiment.
He suggested that I come the following day. I told him, however, that distance is irrelevant with magic, and I would prefer
to work at home. Tolya was intrigued. I decided to fast for
the rest of the day to "replenish my energy." Considering that

every morning I swim in the ice-cold water of a nearby lake followed by yoga, you can imagine how energetically prepared I felt for the task.

At the appointed hour, Tolya called and told me that the patient was sitting in front of him. I began to dance. While dancing, I pictured an abandoned field overgrown with weeds on a collective farm. I knew that this field needed to be plowed; its caretaker had simply forgotten about it. I began searching for the ray of light. Next to the field was a large, beautiful lake. The Chairman of the collective farm was a passionate fisherman, but hadn't had time to fish for quite some time. At that moment, his old friend on the District Committee telephoned him. Everything became clear—it was necessary to get them to go fishing. On the way to the lake, the two friends passed by the field, and the Chairman noticed that the field needed attention. The work was done.

At that point, I began concentrating on the movements of my body and the words I was speaking. After finishing the movements of the dance and receiving the final words (the mantra), I called Tolya to find out the results of the healing work. He exclaimed excitedly that he couldn't believe his eyes. The work which usually required half an hour to complete had been completed in four minutes. Flushed with life, his patient was feeling hot waves of energy flowing through her body from head to toe. I asked Tolya to fill a bottle with water and to "magnetize" it. Then I gave the patient the mantra and instructed her on how to use the mantra and magnetized water. She left very satisfied. Later Tolya told me that the patient was recovering quickly.

Two days later, Tolya arrived with his assistant Rita to witness the miraculous dance. Rita had chosen a client for me. Her husband, Lyonia, had a boil on his rump. His temperature was high, and he had already missed four days of work.

I performed a rousing dance and, perhaps overdoing it, threw myself into a breathtaking somersault along the carpet, which ended with my feet crashing into the door, noisily rattling the stained glass in its window. When the dance was over, a deathly silence hovered over the room for some time. Gradually, the healers pulled themselves together. I magnetized a bottle of water and gave them the standard recommendation on how to use it.

A few days passed, and Tolya called me again. With his characteristic humor, he told me that Lyonia, despite my clear instructions, had immediately drunk all the water at once and, what's more, he had washed it down with beer. A few hours later the boil burst, and the next day Lyonia went back to work.

These two cases were enough to prove to me that magic can be successfully applied to healing. I have had more than enough occasions to reinforce this belief. A young woman at my work, Marina, complained of a severe backache. It was difficult for her to bend forward. I offered to help and performed a dance for her at her home. During this dance, I saw that she was still carrying with her the trauma of her birth. After that, everything proceeded according to the usual script—I gave her the mantra and magnetized water with instructions on how to use them.

Marina called me the next day. She could easily bend forward again without the slightest hint of pain. She also had spoken with her mother about her birth, who told her that it had, in fact, been very difficult.

Marina asked me to work on her husband, Andrey, whom I knew very well. His arm had been hurting him for some time to the point that it was difficult for him to drive. Conventional doctors couldn't help him, and acupuncture gave only temporary relief. Therefore, Andrey was somewhat skeptical when Marina suggested that he try out my treatment—first, because Andrey believed only in conventional medicine; and second, because Andrey and I had worked in the same department for two years. We were friends and often went out together—to the sauna, or to play soccer, chess, or cards. As it is said: "No prophet is accepted in his homeland." How could I heal him when he knew me so well?

In general, it is very difficult to treat close relatives and friends for this very reason. For instance, my mother has asked me several times to prepare magnetized water for her, but it brought her little relief. I think that the reason was that in her subconscious she deeply believed: "I gave birth to him and raised him; I know him inside and out. How is it possible that he can heal people? He would need a special gift for this, but he is just an ordinary person."

On the other hand, my son completely trusts in me as a magician, and so it is quite easy to help him.

When Andrey asked sarcastically over the telephone: "So will I have to guzzle down magic water, too?" I felt I had very little chance of succeeding. However, I decided to try and told Andrey that at 11:00 in the morning the following day I would treat his arm. On the evening after the treatment, he called me again, but his tone had lost its skepticism. This is what had happened: Andrey, of course, had forgotten about our arrangement. However, while driving his car that day, he had noticed that he could easily turn the car to the left, which previously had given him such trouble. His arm didn't hurt! Twisting it into various positions, he became firmly convinced that it was back to normal. He looked at his watch. It was right after 11:00.

Even though his arm was functioning normally, Andrey asked me to magnetize some water for him, just to make sure, which I did. More than three years have since passed, and he no longer complains about his arm at all.

After this, I diligently began practicing healing, until in time I experienced some failures. I was unable to treat the thyroid gland of a relative, and so she turned to a famous psychic. Sometime later, I was unable to save a patient in the final stages of cancer. I understood then that the dance is not a panacea, and with some patients it is necessary to meet over several weeks or months in order to restore their health.

I would like to share some secrets on how to become a healer. First, it is good to complete some kind of course in order to gain self-confidence. Next, you need to muster all your courage and try to actually heal someone. If it works out, it gives you a positive experience to build on. If not, you should pretend that it did. After pretending like this for a while, eventually you will forget that you are pretending, and one day you will succeed.

The further along you go, the easier it gets. A healed patient will recommend you to someone else, and then you will see a small stream of patients gathering who want healing from you. The number will gradually increase until soon the stream becomes a broad, full-flowing river. Then you will have to create an appointment system, which preferably extends several months in advance. When a fortunate patient finally reaches you, he will already be nearly healed, since the healing process actually began when he initially made his appointment.

Here are some thoughts typical of the patient: "This must really be a great master! So many people are trying to see him, and all of them are getting better. That means I will get well, too, when the time comes." So you become a famous healer, and the root of it all is just one successful episode. I would add that, using this same method, you can become a psychologist, wizard, magician, or whatever you like.

Nikolay Kozlov offers a beautiful metaphor about healing in his book *Philosophical Tales*. The basic idea can be summarized as follows: A patient needs theater in order to return to a state of health. If the healer performs the type of theater which the patient needs, then the patient *allows himself* to be healed. These days, there are innumerable types of theater you can use. Following is a list of some of them: taking miraculous pills, or visiting modern clinics which use computers and other elaborate instruments to effect "cures"; you can fast, drink urine, swim in the icy water of a frozen lake, jog, eat only a vegetarian diet, or practice yoga; you might call upon a shaman or magician to remove the contamination within you, or find a psychic who will wave his hands over you; you can sort out your karma, or visit a psychoanalyst who will uncover your suppressed complexes. A comprehensive list of all the various types of theater which can be used for healing would fill several pages.

This relates not only to healing. If you want *to change yourself as a person*, you cannot avoid theater. A person cannot live without theater!

When you finally realize this, why should you even bother consulting a healer at all? Just to have him beguile you, trick you, perform for you? It would be better if you could simply perform the play yourself with you as the only actor. If you yourself are acting in the magical theater, then you have at your disposal tools like thanksgiving, renaming, and dancing. With each success, you gain more experience and self-confidence—just wishing for something suffices to bring it about. However, this can only happen when you are in a state of soaring.

I believe that the state of soaring occurs when *I am applying magical techniques subconsciously*, in the same way as I digest food or walk. This is why the ability to use these techniques in dreams is one of the criteria for mastering the magical arts. In a dream you only have to intend to apply a particular technique, and the situation is instantly transformed. For example, in my dream I am walking along the street without my umbrella, and suddenly it begins pouring rain. As soon as I think about thanksgiving, the rain stops, and the sun is shining brightly in the clear, blue sky. There is no need to recite a monologue.

To end, I will cite one more example of a "miraculous healing."

I became acquainted with Igor on the same day I first learned about thanksgiving. It happened at the summer solstice gathering in Karelia, not far from the town of Pitkyaranta. On the train, I shared a compartment with Andrey, who had recently attended a seminar in magic. He was burning with the desire to share these techniques and during the gathering led an improvised seminar. Workshops held indoors can be very powerful, but when held in the deep forest, their effect is indescribable. It was the time of "White Nights," when it stays light all night long. The full moon was reflected on the still surface of the lake. We were sitting on logs around a crackling fire of fir branches, and Andrey was telling us about the fundamentals of thanksgiving. Suddenly a mysterious stranger appeared at the fire.

He was wearing a long, black coat, and a large, black hat was pulled low over his eyes. A string of dark wooden beads encircled his neck, and beaded bracelets wound round his wrists. He had a thin moustache, a short, sparse beard, and shoulder-length hair. He sat down unpretentiously at the end of a log and drank some tea. After some time, he took out a banjo, pulled the strap around his neck from which dangled a harmonica and various reed pipes, and began to sing.

The song, accompanied by the banjo, would periodically stop abruptly, and he would play on his reeds, or perform a lively dance. Suddenly, the stranger took off his hat and threw it into the fire, but a moment later it was back on his head. He began to improvise freely, composing lyrics and melodies on the spot. For a long time, we were not sure what this fantastic apparition before us was—a dream, a mirage, a real person, or a phantom.

That's how I became acquainted with Igor.

Once he came to Moscow, and we met at the birthday party of one of our friends from the gathering. At the end of the evening, I suggested that we go to a public sauna, but Igor sadly confessed that he had large, itchy pustules all over his body. He couldn't even wear short-sleeve shirts. When I offered him my services, he promised to think about it. He figured, justifiably, that a person should be able to sort out his problems by himself. However, after a couple of days, he called me. I performed a dance, magnetized some water, and gave him a mantra. Soon afterwards, Igor left Moscow.

A year later, I met him again at the summer solstice gathering. Igor was walking around the meadow dressed only in swimming trunks. He casually showed me his smooth skin without a single pustule anywhere.

SHAPE SHIFTER

Dedicated to Grandma Nastya—a night nanny at the nursery school which the author attended as a child—for teaching him to read, and for her harrowing midnight stories about witches and shape shifters.

Tatiana had been attending my group of magicians for some time, and this happy, openhearted woman told the following story:

My friend, Anna, bought a pug dog. When the dog grew up, the breeders encouraged her to enter it into a dog show. It won several gold medals and was invited to enter the International Dog Show.

Anna's mother used to spend summers at her summerhouse, and the dog would go there with her. One day her mother called home: "Your dog is ill; it won't eat anything at all and is trembling constantly." By the following day its condition was even worse. The dog developed sores on its skin, and Anna's mother pulled a swollen tick out of the dog's head.

I told Anna: "It has nothing to do with the tick. It's the gold medals."

"I was thinking that, too," she said. "Who do you think would give her the evil eye?"

"Did you brag about the gold medals to your neighbor, Zoya?"

"Of course, I did!"

"Then that's it! Let's do some work. Can you think of something nice you've done for Zoya?"

"Yes. Zoya once had chronic bronchitis. It was at a time when alternative treatments were illegal, and I took her to an underground group which practiced the breathing methods of Buteyko.* It helped Zoya a lot. She was very pleased and thanked me for it."

"You should repeat this: *'I am the one who takes Zoya to the underground group.'*"

Anna began repeating the name, but in the past tense: "I am the one who took Zoya to the underground group." I explained that she must say it in the present tense, so she started again: "I am taking Zoya to the underground group."

I told her that she shouldn't change the words from the way they were given. Then I recommended: "Repeat this name with your daughter. Let's practice again."

Anna began walking around the room, repeating her new name, and I joined her. Then Anna asked: "How many times should I repeat it?"

"You'll know yourself when to stop. You may feel very light, or it will jolt you."

"Actually, I feel like that already," she said, after repeating the name twice. "My heart immediately stopped aching."

"That's it! The mantra is already working. So you don't need to wait until Sunday (it was Tuesday). Begin repeating it now. When you get to the summerhouse, your dog will be better. Why wait? Repeat it every time you think about your dog, or whenever you see Zoya."

* A Russian professor who developed a system of breathing exercises which is extremely effective with illnesses such as asthma, bronchitis, etc. [trans]

Anna went to her summerhouse that Sunday. The dog was well again, as if there had never been anything wrong with it.

We would like to make here some observations about such concepts as spells, curses, and bewitching with the evil eye. How can my own projection put a spell on me or bewitch me? It can happen only when I forget that I am a magician, when I participate in the dramatic theater of spells and bewitching. In our view, the pathogenic model of the world (or system of beliefs) where bewitching and spells exist is suitable to modern day healers, sorcerers, and wizards. It makes their work with clients much simpler—for example, the client arrives, and the healer explains to him: "Unfortunately, you've been bewitched!" Quite often, by this very phrase he himself is casting a spell on the patient, and then later he removes his own spell.

A majority of healers sincerely believes in this pathogenic theater: "Oh, yes, I can see what this spell looks like. And others, too, see these creatures with their slimy tentacles and suckers. I'll cut them off with my fiery sword!"

The way it works is simple. In the beginning, the healer—a belief in spells being part of his world view—casts a spell. He then sees his own horrible creation, which often he is unable to manage, since he has placed himself in a subordinate position and forgotten that he himself is the author. In fact, the patient, too, can bewitch himself with his own fear and the expectation of being cursed.

Geopathogenic zones have a similar origin—if I believe in their existence and have a dowsing rod in my hands, I cannot help but find them.

When I begin to play in the theater of spells and bewitchment, I automatically forfeit personal responsibility. There are wicked people out there who have bewitched me, and that's why everything is going wrong.

If a magician has a client who truly wants to have a spell removed, the magician must perform his work with a sense of humor, trying to explain how the spell works. The best protection is a smile, the humorous acknowledgement of this process, as in the following most amazing tale narrated by a woman friend who is a healer.

Raya had asked for our help. Her daughter Vera suddenly started fainting, plunging into a state of "non-being" for as long as two or three days. Sometimes she ate nothing; sometimes she would empty the entire refrigerator all at once. When she was conscious, she constantly saw devils with burning eyes, horrifying dungeons, and flying swords. She also heard voices—some would incite her to undertake all manner of heroic deeds; others would call her down to the underworld. Her nightmares and visions didn't leave her even while unconscious, when she was under the power of the devils. And sometimes angels would come down to her, saints appeared, and Mother Mary would cover her with her wings.

The Saints spoke to her through icons, in churches. Sometimes her hand would spontaneously begin writing. The letters which Vera channeled were addressed to her from various beings, and every time in a different handwriting. Everyone wanted her to join their side. The angels told her that she was gifted with divine powers and must serve them, but the devils asserted that she was an amazing witch who could fly on a broomstick. Sometimes when Vera came out of her coma, she could clearly recall everything which had happened to her. Once she had been a beautiful countess chained to a wall in a dark dungeon. Each day she was given only water and a small piece of bread. At times they tortured her mercilessly.

We diagnosed Vera as having a powerful affection of her energetic body. At the time, she was dating a young man named Semyon, who had a daughter from his first marriage. He liked Vera very much, and they planned to marry. Semyon lived with his aunt, who adored his first wife and wanted the family to get back together. His first wife hoped for this as well. We immediately saw the magical spell cast on Vera and Semyon—Semyon's former wife was from Ukraine, and she had evidently turned to Ukrainian sorcerers for help. When Semyon called his ex-wife, she confirmed that this was true, saying that their divorce had been a mistake. She loved Semyon very much and wanted to live with him again.

We sympathized deeply with Vera's situation and pitied her. Now I understand that this pity was a most serious mistake. As we listened to her detailed stories about her visions, we could imagine vividly everything happening to her. We didn't notice how over time we ourselves had started living her nightmares. You might say that we resonated energetically with Vera, and were sharing her reality. The diabolic forces began appearing to us as well.

Vera used to come see us once or twice a week. She first came in March, and by June the situation was completely out of control. Suddenly, like a bolt out of the blue, the word "shape shifter" came to us. My assistant, Tamara, saw an image of Semyon's aunt on the astral plane "flying around at night in a coffin." The aunt's appearance was imposing—her gray hair fluttering in the wind and her hoofed feet jutting horrifyingly out of the coffin. Vera told us that the aunt was a lame hunchback, disabled since childhood, who with difficulty shuffled around the apartment. We remembered the folk tradition that the most powerful witches are hunchbacks and cripples.

Panic seized us. We understood that we were under a deadly threat, that we were facing a battle to the death with dark forces which had united against us. Nobody knows who said it first, but we kept repeating the phrase: "We must survive!"

Vera's father, Victor, went to his summerhouse and experienced two of the most terrifying days of his life. When night fell, something started scraping against the roof, banging on the walls, and scratching at the door. It seemed to Victor that rain was pelting against the window, but outside the weather was clear. Suddenly, the walls began to heat up, becoming quite hot. Victor fled the summerhouse in terror, but it wasn't any better in Moscow. We saw writhing phantoms with burning eyes in dark corners and sparks flew furiously around our apartments. Vera rarely came out of her coma.

The word "shape shifter" had impressed itself on me so much that I began to seriously research the literature for any information I could find. *The Encyclopedia of Mythology* and *The Encyclopedia of Slavic Mythology* told me nothing. I tried to locate the film *The Silver Bullet,** but couldn't find it. My fear increased daily. It seemed that all the powers of Hell were gathering around me, and soon they would start tearing me to pieces.

Finally, I called a friend who is a healer: "Masha, do you know anything about shape shifters?"

"Why, what's happened?"

"I've come across a shape shifter in my practice."

"I can't tell you anything right now. Can you call me tomorrow?"

The next day I called her, and was shocked by her shrill, cracking voice: "Don't you dare call me again! No one can help you with this thing! It's very dangerous. Don't call me!"

---

* A Polish film about a shape shifter. [trans]

So I was left alone, face-to-face with a shape shifter. Every evening after ten o'clock, a murky, grayish-black cloud would appear over the balcony, gradually congealing into an indistinct form—first like a bear with elk's hoofs, then like an elk wearing a bear's skin. It seemed that a scrawny claw would stretch out of the dark cloud, sometimes clutching at my throat, then at my heart. My heart ached unbearably, and nothing would alleviate the pain. My shoulder felt out of joint, and I couldn't fall asleep until two or three in the morning, right before sunrise.

When at last I was able to lie down to sleep, I would put a large icon of Jesus Christ under my pillow. On one side I placed the Bible which I had taken with me to Jerusalem and had lain upon our Lord's coffin; on the other side I placed a crucifix. I kept candles burning constantly, and a fire could easily have started, since the candles would burn down and topple over as I slept. I could fall asleep for only about fifteen minutes, and then I'd jump up with a start, take hold of the Bible and crucifix, and press my forehead to the icon. Then I would lie back down and try to calm myself. This continued throughout the rest of the night.

In the morning Tamara would come over. She told me how her balcony had been rocking up and down, and how she had prayed constantly all night long, with a candle in one hand and a cross in the other. She made the sign of the cross over everything, moving the candles around in such a frenzy that by morning she could barely feel her hands. The candles would crackle and sputter, emitting a dense, black smoke which rose up to the ceiling. One day, Tamara reported dreadfully that the previous evening all of her icons had suddenly fallen off the shelf. By the end of that night, Tamara had learned by heart almost the entire book of prayers, reciting one prayer after another. She could recite without stumbling such complicated prayers as "To the Resuscitating Cross" and Psalm 91 "He who dwelleth in the shelter of the Most High."

I was in a crazed state and have no idea how I was able to function. All five of us—Tamara, Vera, Raya, Victor, and I—often met together and talked to each other by phone. We could think of nothing else. We kept asking each other: "How're you getting on?" And our reports about attacks sounded more and more like war dispatches. In fact, quite often I literally was fighting a war, concentrating rays of light in the center of my palms and blasting the dark cloud with them. This would drive the cloud back, or shrink it, or contain it, as I tried desperately to send it back into antimatter. The cloud might disappear for a while, but it always came back.

My mother stopped sleeping during the night, and her heart seizures became more frequent. My son would kick and cry out in his sleep, and he had constant nightmares. Tamara's mother fell down and broke her leg, which we blamed on an "incursion" of enemy powers. Her father's bladder completely failed for a time, and he had to check into a hospital. Raya developed problems with her liver and kidneys, and Victor's psoriasis flared up. It felt like we had encountered an invincible power. I counted the days to my vacation when I could get away, but I kept thinking in the back of my mind: "Where can I possibly escape to? It'll follow me anywhere, even to Pitsunda!"

At one point, we turned to an Orthodox priest, but he simply exhorted us to live in the blessed love of our Lord, and to pray from morning to night; then it would go away by itself. But already we were surviving only by our constant prayers.

The time came for our vacation to the Black Sea, but Vera was in such a terrible state that we couldn't leave her behind. Vera's parents also were afraid to stay in Moscow, defenseless against the shape shifter without our prayers and battle-rays of light. I suggested that they, too, come with us, and together we would beat back the shape shifter in Pitsunda.

Then, only three days before our flight, I felt as if I suddenly woke up from a nightmare. I called my fellow magicians, and we arranged a group meeting—two magicians, Vera, Tamara, my other assistant, and me. The magicians suggested that we apply the technique known as *group phantom,** explaining: "It is obvious that the aunt lacks tranquility and warmth of heart, which is not surprising considering that she has been disabled since early childhood. She probably has led a very hard life. What's more, you have clothed her in a pathological image, developing this image over a long period of time in your group mind. Now we will have to 'change her clothes.'"

The magicians suggested that we stand in a circle holding hands. The aunt was summoned to the center of the circle, and we started sending her imaginary pictures. Someone would suggest an image, and the rest of us developed it further, adding details. We gave her a meadow filled with flowers, a mystery novel, ginseng, a quilted jacket with gold buttons, a thoroughbred horse and carriage, and many other gifts. In time, the hunchbacked old woman transformed into a cute little girl, three or four years old, playing happily with her jump rope. We mentally hugged this girl, pressing her close to our hearts and stroking her hair. The magicians suggested that we sing a song for her which they recently had learned at a gathering:

> May the Sun of our love illuminate all,
> May the warmth of our hearts give us life,
> May singing and laughter bring joy to the world,

---

* In this book we have not described this powerful technique, but one can get a general idea about it from the story.

So all people may live without strife.
Om, Om, Om, Om.

The melody was very beautiful, and we sang the verse with
deep feeling about ten times. Tears welled up in my eyes. At
last the magicians announced that it was enough, and a deep
silence settled over us, which no one wanted to break for a
long time. For the first time in three months, I felt calm and
happy. The magicians declared that, if we wanted to live in
peace, we would have to sing this song regularly.

All seven of us left on our vacation together—Vera, her
parents, Tamara, and me along with my son and my friend
Liusia. For the first two days of vacation, we didn't think at
all about the shape shifter or the song. The weather was marvelous, the sea was warm and calm, and the golden sands of
the beach gladdened our hearts. Lush greenery flourished
everywhere—it had rained the week before our arrival—and
the valley was chock full of fragrant, blossoming flowers.
We picked eggplants in the garden just a few steps from our
kitchen and cooked them up fresh.

When we would walk to the sea, we had to pass by two
small marshes. Two gigantic pigs were often wallowing leisurely in the mud, and we often stopped to admire them. You
could tell how much the pigs loved it there. We could feel
their bliss, and this cheered us up. If for some reason the pigs
were absent, frogs showed up instead. They would slowly rise
to the surface and float there with their noses sticking out,
gently swishing their webbed feet. Some of them dived down
to putter about the bottom.

There was yet another interesting spot on the way to the
sea—a bridge crossed over a small, swift-flowing stream, and
right below the bridge were several pools. Fish circled around
in the water. We used to sit on this bridge and forget about

everything as we watched the fish shimmering in the patches
of sunlight. Time simply stopped.

When we finally moved on toward the sea, we passed the
key point on the entire route—an iron pipe from which water
poured out under high pressure. Here the local Armenians
washed their cars; this place was their "clubhouse," where the
"real men" of the valley gathered. Of course, all of them wore
the same flat caps.

Next to the pipe was the electrical switchbox for the entire
valley. An elderly Armenian man kept watch over it. His job
was to move the switch handle up or down from time to time.
Sometimes he tightened some kind of screw as well. This
switch "operator" was one of the most respected elders in the
valley, and his words held weight in local disputes. It was interesting that neither the striking, full-figured Tamara, nor I,
with my curvaceous body, nor Raya, an interesting, mature
woman, nor the slender, ethereal Liusia attracted the attention of this Armenian. He only had eyes for emaciated little
Vera with dark circles under her eyes and tangled jet-black
hair. Vera is, in fact, very attractive, but at that time she looked
terminally ill. But whenever we passed the elderly Armenian
on the way to the beach, he would point his thick hairy finger
at her and exclaim: "Ah! Whata girla!"

Our holidays were going fine until one morning our landlady came in to tell us that Vera was not looking well. I ran to
her room. Vera was doubled over on her bed. She was wheez-
ing and shaking all over, causing her feet to kick lightly against
the bed. Tamara and I instantly started trying to pull her out
of her state with our usual methods: waving our hands over
her, directing flows of energy and light. Then Liusia came in
and began singing "The Sun of Love." We happily joined in.
Vera was sweating profusely, but finally her body straightened
out, and she fell asleep for about an hour and a half. Suddenly,

she started screaming—she had glimpsed something through the window. We responded by heartily singing "The Sun of Love." You might say that we were repelling Vera's final attempt to draw us back into that apocalyptic horror film we had been living.

Four days passed, and Raya, Victor, and I went mushroom hunting in the mountains. We were walking through a deep canyon littered with fallen trees—sometime before there had been a mud slide which had knocked down the trees, but they were all dried out now. Sharp spikes of broken branches stuck out like swords in all directions, interrupted here and there by huge boulders. It felt like we were walking through a fantastic fairyland. Then Raya said: "It's been a long time since anything has happened. There have been no visitations at all."

At that moment, Raya cut her leg on a sharp knot. I immediately filled the valley with the sounds of "The Sun of Love."

Vera was better through the rest of our vacation; nothing haunted her. Sometimes she felt a bit nauseated, but, for the first time in many years, her digestion became regular, and she began to eat normally.

In the late afternoons, we would stroll along the seashore. Usually Vera walked in front, followed by each of us in turn at intervals of about thirty yards. This created the illusion of being alone with all of nature. I would walk at the very edge of the water, feeling the soft sand under my feet, collecting unusual stones, pieces of glass, and wood molded by the sea into interesting shapes. I quietly sang to myself "The Sun of Love" absolutely certain that the others were also singing this same hymn.

When I returned to Moscow, I was overjoyed that the nightmares had ceased. Everything had returned to normal. I knew that I had learned never again to be drawn into such a nightmare.

A MEDICAL ENIGMA

Several years ago, during a routine medical examination, a tumor was discovered growing in my supposedly healthy body.* In general, I try not obsess over every sore spot and minor ailment if I can alleviate them with medication. This time, though, I was seriously worried, and the doctor's prognosis didn't make me any more optimistic.

At that same time, I gave birth to my child, only increasing my nervousness. The tumor began to bother me more and became painful. The doctors were extremely straightforward, describing in no uncertain terms the tragic consequences if the process was not stopped in time. They offered only one way out—surgical intervention. I just had to choose between the scalpel and laser. Both these options sent me into a state of inner panic.

Due to my training in practical magic, I hesitated to surrender to the hands of a surgeon. Recent successes applying magical techniques to my life had encouraged me so much that I decided to heal myself.** I carefully analyzed the period

* This story is narrated by a young woman. [trans]

** The magical achievements of our heroine began with her success in freeing herself from psychological issues which had tormented her for years. With the help of renaming—*"I am the one who wraps Vitka in toilet paper"*—in just half an hour she rid herself of devastating fears which had developed into a persecution complex.

of time right before the first symptoms appeared. This research revealed the root episode.

At the age of eleven, I was short and chubby and loved to eat. However, I was very distressed by my weight and passionately dreamed of becoming slim. So when our Physical Education teacher opened up enrollment in track and field, I didn't think twice about signing up. I wasn't attracted to the sport at all, but beauty demanded sacrifices. I gave up my favorite painting class and forced myself to pump iron, suppressing my natural desire to enjoy a good meal. In the end, I never became a sports star, but after six years I did acquire a strong aversion to track and field.

The price I paid for a slender figure was too high. What's more, my sacrifice was in vain, as I would have slimmed down with age anyway, without the exhaustive training and strict diet. I now understand that I was replaying that old script all over again. I was trying to suppress the ailment to get rid of it by force. In my childhood, I loved fried potatoes with brown, crispy crusts, but they were forbidden fruit during my struggle against fat. So I chose the name: *"I am the one who devours fried potatoes."*

As soon as I began this work, I felt great relief and realized that I had freed myself from inner tension accumulated over many years. For ten days I conscientiously embodied my new image. When I went to the clinic for my next appointment, a new doctor examined me. He surprised me with the question: "What am I supposed to be looking for?" I showed him the results of my previous examination, and the perplexed doctor uttered: "So you've had the operation already?" I shook my head. His next comment revealed a mix of genuine astonishment and sarcasm: "So I guess it simply disappeared on its own." I grabbed the results of the medical exam and ran out of his office, avoiding the questions clearly written on the faces of the medical personnel all around.

I only managed to pull myself together and rethink my entire situation when I had plopped down on a bench in a city square and lit up a cigarette. My quick healing had happened against all expectations. In the depths of my heart, I conceded the possibility that the doctor might have made a mistake, and went to get a second opinion from another doctor. The result was the same. The tumor, which had been oppressing me and stealing my peace of mind, had simply disappeared. My joy was so great that I feared for my very sanity. And now, although my tongue itches to tell my friends about this miraculous healing, what little remains of my common sense has sealed my chattering lips.

GOLDILOCKS

My old friend and schoolmate, Sergey, telephoned me from a city down south to tell me that his three-year old daughter, Katya, was rapidly losing her hearing. The doctors diagnosed her as having bilateral acoustic neuritis. This is a severe condition, and no medicine or therapy would help. The girl's hearing was progressively becoming worse. An urgent operation was recommended, but it could only be performed at one of Moscow's research clinics using a recently developed procedure. However, in order to get an appointment for the operation, it was necessary to first have a preliminary examination, and appointments were fully booked for the next two months. Katya couldn't wait that long.

There is no such thing as a hopeless situation for a magician. In fact, clients do not even have to be present in order to work with them; they can be thousands of miles away. When Katya was very little, I had given her a big doll with golden hair. Goldilocks had appealed to me more than all the other dolls in the toy store and had won Katya's heart as well. Sergey told me that the doll had become one of her favorite toys.

I immediately began whirling in a fluent and graceful dance. This gradually changed into broad, sweeping movements with my body, which abruptly stopped, shifting into vigorous leaps through the air. The soundtrack also changed rapidly with the movements, ending with the mantra YALLA BIKUNCHA RAPALLUK.

After the dance, I felt an unusual suppleness. Every cell of my body was electrified, filled with life-giving energy. Then I turned to the doll and entrusted her with an important task—to transmit good health to the girl by means of this mantra.

I couldn't help but recall the main character of the well-known Russian fairytale, Vasilisa the Beautiful. She always kept her favorite doll close to her and treated it to tasty morsels of food. Whenever misfortune befell Vasilisa—say, her stepmother piled housework onto her—the doll would help with her chores. While Vasilisa rested in the shade picking flowers, the doll would weed the vegetable garden, water the cabbages, fetch water from the well, and replenish the stove with firewood.

Besides the doll, I utilized magnetized water, which works particularly well because it is in constant contact with the client. You can drink it, use it for cooking, for washing, and taking a bath. I placed a bottle of water in front of me and "downloaded" the mantra into it. You can further galvanize this process by imagining that inside each particle of water a tiny, bearded man performs the last movement of the dance while singing the mantra. To replenish the supply of this miraculous water, you pour regular water into what remains of the magnetized water, shake it thoroughly, and the healing qualities are transmitted to the entire contents.

It is noteworthy that this procedure allows you to actually alter the physical and chemical qualities of the water. The magnetized water will retain its freshness and flavor for many years. One of my clients told me that she had inadvertently left her jar of magnetized water at her summerhouse during a severe cold spell. When she returned for it several days later, she couldn't believe her eyes—the water hadn't even frozen!

One of Sergey's relatives worked as a conductor on the Moscow train to his city. I delivered her the bottle with detailed instructions on how to use the water and mantra. I suggested to Sergey that he make a game of it with his daughter, telling her that while she slept a good fairy had flown to her from a distant land to bring her the "water of life." The fairy had asked Goldilocks to take care of Katya and had given the doll "magic words" (the mantra) to heal her. Little Katya liked this game very much, pressing her parents for all the particulars of the fairy's visit. She was constantly talking to her doll and every night took it to bed with her, hugging Goldilocks close to her heart. Sergey and his wife conscientiously repeated the "spell" and sprinkled the magnetized water everywhere. Katya loved drinking it as well.

After about three weeks, Sergey telephoned me very worried. He told me that everything was going well—he no longer had to shout loudly into Katya's ear—but another problem had arisen. The little girl had inadvertently drunk up all of the water; the bottle was completely empty. I laughed and simply presented Sergey with an alternate world view. Just one drop is plenty—even a single molecule of the "elixir" on the bottom of the bottle—to magnetize any added water. Besides, the bottle itself has been magnetized as well. After any new water is poured in, you can see those dignified bearded fellows solemnly descending the walls of the bottle into the water, magnetizing it with healing energy. The problem was solved.

Time passed, and Katya's hearing gradually was restored. Goldilocks was her constant companion. The last time I spoke with Sergey, he confirmed that Katya could hear perfectly normally, which had been quite a surprise to the doctors.

THE SLINGSHOT

My wife's colleague at work, Darya Andreevna, asked me for help. She complained about a sharp pain in her right arm. Every so often, the pain would shoot from her wrist up to her shoulder joint. The doctors could not give her any definite diagnosis, alluding to her age and shrugging their shoulders.

While she was describing her ailment, I closed my eyes mysteriously. Darya Andreevna appeared to me as a wild, mischievous little girl in a faded, flowery dress, holding a large slingshot in her hand. Pulling back its long, grey band, she was skillfully shooting rotten tomatoes in every direction.

After describing this image to my client, I recommended that she repeat the name: *"I am the one who shoots rotten tomatoes."* While doing this, she should visualize the corresponding image. Darya Andreevna chose not to take my advice to construct a real slingshot in consideration of the peace of mind of those around her. So I advised her to imitate the v-shape of a slingshot using the index and middle fingers of her left hand, and with her right hand to pull back an imaginary band loaded with a rotten tomato. Darya Andreevna deftly performed this motion.

After our meeting, Darya Andreevna was often spotted by her colleagues doing this strange exercise. Secretly, so as not to attract attention, she would pretend to shoot off the slingshot. One woman accidentally witnessed this spectacle, and it bothered her for a long time. When she finally found out what was going on, she became extremely upset. One night,

when I came to pick up my wife at work, she discreetly enquired: "Would it hurt someone if Darya Andreevna shot a
person in the face with a tomato?" (We are unsure of the reasons for her worries, but possibly the woman had heard stories
about well-intending citizens becoming victims of curses and
spells.) Trying my best to keep a straight face, I reassured her
that the tomatoes were completely harmless, and she sighed
deeply in relief.

However, let's return to our "sharpshooter." Darya Andreevna's arm gradually bothered her less and less. Before
long, the pain had disappeared completely and never came
back.

A ONE DAY CURE FOR THE FLU

When one of my patients, Nina Ivanovna, arrived for a massage, she had a terrible cold. She was sneezing, sniffling, and coughing.

"I'm really sick," she said dejectedly through clogged sinuses. "My nose is running horribly. It's probably the flu. I heard that there's an awful bug going around Moscow, from Hong Kong. Last night, when I went to bed, I felt that something wasn't right; my nose was itchy, and I had the chills. By morning I had a full-blown flu and soaring temperature. Now I'll be laid up for a week. You know what they say: with the flu, if you don't treat it, it'll last for a week, and if you do treat it, it'll last seven days."

Nina Ivanovna was a trained magician and knew how to give thanks to Vanya. So I asked her: "Why didn't you thank the disease right away?"

She shrugged her shoulders. "I just forgot that I could do that."

Now that she remembered her magic wand, Nina Ivanovna gave thanks to her illness. Here is her passionate declaration: "My dear and most honorable flu! I realize that you have completed a long and difficult journey from Hong Kong. My darling, thank you so much!"

Then she described to me the image of the gift she was offering to her dear guest from Hong Kong. It was a large, bizarrely-shaped seashell with toothed edges. The outside of the shell was rippled, beige-colored, with an intricate, textured design. The inside was coated with a thin layer of mother-of-pearl. Atop its transparent, gelatinous flesh rested a pastel pink, frosted pearl. Nina Ivanovna was utterly enchanted by this vision. She kept repeating joyfully: "I can't believe I managed to dream up such a beautiful gift!" After all, she had just been doubting that she could imagine any suitable picture at all.

All this work took only a few minutes. Suddenly, Nina Ivanovna exclaimed in surprise: "You know what? I can breathe through my nose again!"

As we parted, I reminded her that, instead of pills and medicines, she should concentrate on her remarkable pearl. The next day, a cheerful and satisfied Nina Ivanovna returned for her routine massage. She told me that last night she had felt much better, and by morning her temperature was back to normal. The flu was completely gone.

Magicians on holiday

Vacation in the Crimea

My wife and I have a favorite place on the southern shore of the Crimea. This year, too, we were planning to travel there. But there was one problem—my wife needed to get time off from her work in the beginning of September. Previously, she had taken her vacation during the summer, and there had been no problem. One day my wife came home from work very upset. She said that the summer vacation schedule had been drawn up, and in September, their busiest month, there was no one to fill in for her. With tears in her eyes, Lenulia explained that all her colleagues had already chosen the best times for their vacations. Only she had been left out.

The following day we went to the woods. On the shore of a lake, in a small glade surrounded by mighty birches, I started dancing. These dances are usually very expressive, and performing them in city apartments can be constricting. More than once, I have collided with a ceiling lamp, a bed, or something else. In the expanse of the forest, however, I can spread out as much as I want. The sound of the final mantra LUNCHISUR had hardly died out, echoing through the forest, when Lenulia tried to squeeze out of me the reason for the dance. I didn't tell her that the dance had been dedicated to her vacation time. She had already given up on the idea of a September vacation in the Crimea, and she would have been skeptical and mistrustful of my efforts.

After this, whenever we would talk about our vacation, I repeated the mantra within, trying to calm my wife and instill confidence in her. But the news from her work was not comforting. Once someone told her: "Even the bosses don't take vacations in September." Another time she complained that vacation times had been scheduled so tightly that she probably wouldn't get any at all that summer. In the meantime, summer came, and I went away to a solstice gathering for a couple weeks. By the time I returned at the end of June, the problem had resolved itself. It turned out that one of Lenulia's co-workers wanted to take her vacation in July and had agreed to fill in for Lenulia at the beginning of September.

Occasionally my wife would become anxious, saying things like: "It'll probably all fall through." It had come together too easily. Because of this, I still repeated LUNCHISUR as needed. I finally revealed to her the mystery of the dance in September, in the woods under the gentle Crimean sun, but it wasn't that surprising to her. She had long suspected that it never could have worked out so easily without the help of magic.

Magic also played an essential role in our first trip together to the Crimea. The underlying motto for that trip was: "May everything go wrong!" Our destination was an amazingly beautiful hideaway in the Crimea—a village named Novy Svet near the town of Sudak. As always, it was very difficult to get railway tickets to this blessed land. But luck smiled on us, and the ticket cashier somehow managed to come up with two second-class tickets on the train from Moscow to Feodosia—there were none at all to Simferopol. However, these coveted tickets turned out to be the very worst seats on the train car, right next to the toilet. As is usually the case, the toilet was never cleaned out, so we were constantly treated to its enduring aroma for the entire journey. Yet the smell, the incessant slamming of the bathroom door, and the endless flow of people were nothing compared to what was to come.

At the glorious city of Tula, a new passenger entered the car and sat down opposite us. He was extremely drunk and could barely talk. As soon as the train started off, he extracted a bottle of vodka from the depths of his old, worn-out brief-case, followed by a rock-hard chunk of Tula's famous spice bread. None of the passengers accepted his offer for a drink or for spice bread. Mumbling something like: "Well, f... all of you then," our Tula patriot knocked back a glass of vodka and tried to bite off a piece of spice bread. But the bread wouldn't yield, and the fellow, completely frustrated, decided to climb up onto his upper berth. After three or four attempts, he finally managed to conquer his "Bastille," and peace settled over the train car, occasionally disturbed by his loud snoring. As it turned out, this was the quiet before the storm.

At about 7:00 that evening, a sudden bang shook the entire car. No, it wasn't the drunkard crashing down from his upper bunk. Someone had thrown a large stone through our window! Shards of glass scattered everywhere. Amazingly, nobody was hurt. Startled by the noise, passengers from the whole train car came running over. They offered various explanations ranging from hooliganism of the local kids to a political terrorist act connected with the division of the Black Sea fleet at the break-up of the Soviet Union. All this noise woke up our friend from Tula. He was extremely agitated and, finishing his bottle of vodka, became actively involved in the discussion. Gradually, everyone went back to their seats. Night fell, and the passengers prepared for bed.

However, our inebriated gentleman, impassioned by events, clearly wasn't going back to sleep. He sat on the lower bunk of a young woman and, talking incessantly, began flirting with her. She did not respond with mutual feelings, and our don

Juan responded with a renewed assault. None of our threats or admonitions worked—he would stop for a few moments, and then start mumbling something, chastising his victim for not loving her neighbor and various other transgressions. On top of this, a cold wind was whistling through the broken window. There was no way we could fall asleep. I had temporarily forgotten my abilities as a magician.

Finally, the knocking of the wheels and the monotonous rocking of the carriage lulled me to sleep. When I finally awoke, the windbag was gone. Lenulia, who had not slept a wink, said that he had stopped talking right before dawn. We got off the train at the station "Aivazovskaya," one stop before Feodosia. The bus depot was located next to the train station, but again we were obstructed—the next bus to Sudak wouldn't leave for four hours. Taxi drivers, who were milling lazily about the square in front of the station, were charging exorbitant prices. To pass the time, we walked to the beach and, after a long swim, returned to the bus station.

The bus ride was remarkably picturesque as we passed through the resort of Koktebel and the Valley of the Sun. However, my wife couldn't enjoy the views. She had fallen asleep after her long, sleepless night on the train. At last we arrived in Sudak. We had only four miles left until our final destination—the small village of Novy Svet. But again we were delayed by a long break between buses. We didn't want to wait for two whole hours, so we took a taxi. On the way, the driver told us that he had friends in the village who could help us find accommodations—Galya worked at a resort hotel, and Rita rented out her room to tourists.

When we stepped out of the car, a tropical shower poured down on us. Although the five-storey apartment building where Rita lived was only a few steps away, we got soaked to the bone. Rita wasn't home. We managed to find out from her neighbors that she would arrive home from work soon. We waited in the entryway for about an hour. The rain was coming down in buckets, so we couldn't go out at all. In the end, our hopes didn't materialize—Rita refused to rent out her room. When the rain finally stopped, I set out for the resort on the other side of town.

At the hotel, Galya raised her hands in dismay. "There's nothing I can do for you. July is peak season, and all our rooms are full. And not just our hotel. There are so many tourists now that there are no rooms anywhere. Try private apartments. Maybe you'll get lucky."

I had little hope that we would find a room since the village is very small. There are only a few large apartment complexes. I went from one building to the next, trying to find a room to rent, but everywhere signs were posted: "Please do not inquire. There are no rooms (apartments) for rent here". When I finally reached the last building, I realized I had hit a dead end. The sun was sinking lower. Faced with the depressing prospect of spending the night on the beach, I went back to my wife. She, too, was utterly discouraged. I had to do something quick, and only then, when I was pushed up against the wall by circumstances, did I suddenly remember: "I'm a magician! How could I forget?" As the Russian proverb says: "A man won't cross himself until lightening strikes!"

I seized this opportunity, as a drowning man clutches at a piece of straw. Sitting down on a bench, I closed my eyes and began my monologue: "Thank you, dear Vanya, for reminding me that I am a magician. I offer you a sleek sailing ship with bright red sails. On the deck sailors are sitting around a fire baking potatoes."

After replenishing ourselves with some food, I set off for the citadel of our last hope—a zigzag-shaped five-storey apartment building. The image of the ship with bright red sails remained fixed in my mind. After checking out one entryway, I decided to move on to the next. Right as I entered the first-floor corridor, I bumped into a suntanned man in his forties.

"Looking for a room, are you?" he addressed me. "My girlfriend and I are leaving town in about half an hour. You should talk to my landlord."

The room was clean and spacious with two beds, an armchair, table, and cupboard. The balcony looked out on a fabulous view of Mounts Sokol and Orel which rose up on either side of the bay. The rent was quite reasonable, and we were soon unpacking our things.

I had first visited Novy Svet five years before, and ever since then it has enthralled my heart. My wife and I prefer swimming at Czar's Beach. There are two ways to get there—by a narrow goat trail winding down from Skvoznoy Grotto, or along the bottom of a narrow canyon. It was quicker and easier to take the canyon route. On the first day of our vacation, we ran into an obstacle in the form of the local forest warden.

My initial introduction to him had occurred during my first visit to the Crimea. Adjacent to Novy Svet is a nature preserve. My friend Kostya and I had put up our tent in a secluded valley on the slope of Mount Sokol. The next morning we went down to swim in Razboinik Bay. In the late afternoon, we suddenly heard loud shouts and whistling coming from above us on the Golytsin Trail. A man was shouting and waving his arms indignantly. However, he did not come down, and we continued to bliss out on the beach. When we climbed up the trail later to return to our camp, the man, like some mysterious apparition, leaped out from behind a rocky crag. He looked very much like a bandit—straggly black hair and beard and an angry face with spittle at the edges of his toothless mouth. This solemn champion of the natural world presented us his warden's badge and started threatening us with a fine. We pretended that this was the first time we had ever heard about the nature preserve. Then several more people appeared on the trail, and the warden rushed toward them, fiercely blowing his whistle. With that, my first encounter with the warden was over.

Not suspecting anything, Lenulia and I walked through the juniper grove in order to get down to the canyon which led to Czar's Beach. Seemingly right out of the ground, the figure of the warden rose up before us, shouting: "Well, well, well. And where are we off to?" Without any attempt to be polite, the warden told us to clear out while we could. We decided to resort to guerilla tactics. We turned around, made a large loop, and then descended to the canyon. When we were only fifty yards from Czar's Beach, the booming voice of the omnipresent warden rang out from the top of the canyon. There was nothing we could do—we went down instead to the public beach. The next day we were not ambushed, but the following day the warden appeared again. This time he wasn't alone but with his assistant. They showed up in the middle of the day right there on Czar's Beach. The tourists were given the choice of paying a fee to remain in the preserve or to get out.

I thanked the warden for warning me that for the rest of our vacation we would have to swim at the noisy, overcrowded public beach, and I gave him a large Venetian flask filled with a healing ointment which exuded an erotic fragrance. The flask was wrapped in willow wicker.

After that, a blessed peace settled over Czar's Beach. Only once more did we meet the warden. He was stumbling along the shoreline, which led me to think somewhat differently about the contents of that flask.

With only a few days left of our vacation, we decided to climb Mount Sokol (1562 ft). Even though we didn't reach the peak, for Lenulia it was quite a feat. The last few steps demanded an unprecedented effort from her, but she was rewarded beyond all measure. A glorious panorama stretched out before us—Novy Svet, Sudak, the Genoese fortress, beautiful bays, and tree-covered mountains. The setting sun shone with an inimitable play of light and shadow, making everything around us stand out in vivid color. We felt like we had entered a fairyland. An energetic wave rose up from the depths of the mountain and passed through our bodies. It seemed that at any moment I would take off and fly off into the heavens. Lenulia was very proud of her triumph, and later she liked to tell her friends how she had climbed Mount Sokol "with her tongue hanging over her shoulder." Her fantastic state of being was fixed in the name: *"I am the one who climbs Mount Sokol."* And this name always works for her without fail even up to this day.

All in all, we had a wonderful vacation and returned home filled with vibrant memories. In comparison, the difficulties which we had experienced at the beginning of our journey have long since faded away. Yet, by using magic, these unnecessary problems could have been avoided. Our next trip to Novy Svet confirmed this.

Having learned through bitter experience, I was well-prepared for our next vacation, early on dedicating a dance to it. The mantra had a beautiful, melodic sound—EY YANUZA TURALUKALAPA. This short refrain would ensure a most favorable journey—a comfortable train ride, timely bus connections, available accommodations, good living conditions, sunny weather, and so on.

This time we were traveling with friends—a married couple and their son. The train car was neat and tidy, and both toilets were functioning. We reached Simferopol without incident. On the platform, the "Grand Marshal" waved his arm to signal the start of the parade, proclaiming: "Let the mantra begin!" Singing out TURALUKALAPA, the procession set off for the bus depot. While Dmitry and I were studying the timetable, a bright, young man appeared out of nowhere, offering us a ride in his beige Volga. His price was just a bit more than bus tickets, so we agreed without thinking twice.

Everything happened so fast that we were somewhat taken aback. Our wives didn't even have time to buy some fresh fruit. Our driver rushed us straight to Novy Svet. When we arrived, our car was instantly surrounded by a swarm of old ladies, vying to rent us rooms and cottages. We barely managed to escape them and went straight to Vasilievna, our landlady from the previous summer. She had two rooms available, and we rented both of them. Vasilievna complained that, despite it being peak season (the middle of July), there were very few tourists this year. The locals couldn't remember such a summer.

We spent our first few days on Czar's Beach. Our old friend, the warden, didn't turn up, although a couple times we glimpsed someone who looked a lot like him high up on the ridge. Strolling along Cape Kapchik, we climbed to the top and spied a small secluded beach below. A few women were picturesquely sunbathing naked there. We had found it—the promised land! The descent to the beach took us down a steep slope of volcanic rock, which was why there were so few people there. The beach was well sheltered from the wind by cliffs. In an expression of solidarity with the suntanned nymphs, we took off all our clothes. Dmitry sighed sorrowfully as he looked at them: "It's like bringing coals to Newcastle!" We admired the huge rocks which jutted out of the water. We dove in with masks and swam around the rocks

to our heart's content, chasing crabs and enjoying the under-
water kingdom. This inconspicuous little beach became our
favorite haunt. On the day we discovered it, a curious incident
occurred.

The sun had set behind the high cliff, so we started heading home. Without hurrying, we climbed up the slope to the
ridgeline of Cape Kapchik. When we reached level ground,
I looked up and winced. A few steps away, our unforgettable
warden was sitting under a juniper bush. "So much for that
beach!" was my first thought. Seeing us coming, he slowly
stood up and came over to us. As it turned out, this terror of
tourists was a bit tipsy. We cautiously stepped closer and, to
be on the safe side, politely greeted him. Imperiously stretch-
ing forth his arm toward Czar's Beach, he winked conspira-
torially and asked our advice: "Should I go kick them out? I
really don't feel like walking all the way down there." I stood
rooted to the spot and, unable to reply, simply shrugged my
shoulders. The warden followed us for a little way, complain-
ing how the tourists were always leaving trash on the beach.
Then he trotted down to Czar's Beach. He never crossed our
path again.

MUSHROOM HUNTING

The vacation season in Novy Svet was quite rainy that year, and the marketplace was full of field mushrooms. For an inveterate mushroom hunter like myself, the sight of someone else's buckets filled with succulent, juicy mushrooms was like salt on a wound. When Vasya, the twelve-year-old son of our landlady, brought home half a bag of boletus and field mushrooms, my patience ran out.

I had a friendly relationship with Vasya. I taught him how to add and subtract fractions, and he showed me a place along the shoreline which had an abundance of crabs. The following story illustrates the trust which had grown between us.

Once Vasya confided in me a frightful secret. With a conspiratorial look, he drew out from under his shirt an old, rusted-out Soviet grenade from World War II. His older brother, Sergey, had found it in a juniper thicket on Mount Sokol. Now they were hiding it in their home in strict secrecy from their mother. Seeing how carelessly Vasya was tossing the grenade up in the air, I started fitfully thanking Vanya.

Vasya handed me his dangerous toy. I examined it very carefully and noticed that the hole for the pin was completely rusted up and caked over with mud. Vasya said: "Too bad there's no pin. Maybe it won't explode. But don't worry, I won't blast it off by myself. Sergey promised to take me with him to blow it up somewhere in the mountains." I handed the grenade back to Vasya and advised him to return it to its hiding place. He reluctantly took it back.

It wasn't particularly difficult to extract from Vasya where the secret mushroom patches were generally located, although the final destination was described rather vaguely (perhaps on purpose). The next morning I woke up early. The day was overcast, and I was glad that I wasn't tempted to go off swimming, so I could hunt for mushrooms in the mountains with a clear conscience.

However, my cheerful mood was premature—right as I was leaving, a heavy downpour interrupted my plans. I urgently had to change the weather. After about fifteen minutes, the rain became lighter and, ignoring my wife's warnings, I set out. Picking my way between rocky torrents, I rapidly ascended along the dilapidated Czar's Highway. It snaked between thick layers of limestone which stuck up out of the ground, skirting the trunks of ancient pines. The air was filled with the pungent smell of pine needles. Below me opened up a breathtaking view of Zelenaya Bay, Novy Svet, and Mounts Sokol and Orel, which majestically flanked either side of the bay.

Not far from the top, I met up with a group of local kids also hunting mushrooms. They were soaked from head to toe. Their buckets were nearly empty, and the thought flashed through my mind: "If these little imps, who know the local area inside and out, couldn't find any mushrooms, what hope do I have?"

Then I remembered my magical abilities. I gave thanks to the children for warning me that my worries could materialize, and I would end up with no mushrooms at all, even if I searched everywhere around Novy Svet, or even the whole of the Crimean peninsula. I offered the children a bronze crocodile head with eyes of green peas.

After a while, I found myself at the bottom of a ravine not far from the place described by Vasya. From that point, I had to walk along the ravine, and then up a slope where the mushrooms supposedly grew. But the ravine stretched on for a long way, and it wasn't clear exactly where I should start upward. I clambered up a slope covered with a dense overgrowth of hornbeam and Crimean scrub oak. Drops of water showered down on me from the trees, and soon I was soaking wet. I still hadn't found a single mushroom. Finally, I was forced to return to the bottom of the ravine, my sneakers slipping and squishing through the muddy clay soil.

Contemplating the vagaries of mushroom hunting, I recalled a wonderful magical technique. I stopped, looked around, and greeted the spirit of the local woods.* I thanked it and, closing my eyes, tried to picture the spirit in my imagination. In my mind's eye, I painted an image of a watchtower made of grey bricks flying on a magic carpet. I asked the spirit of the woods what it would like added to this image. Then I began to complete the picture: the tower was decorated with multi-colored flags and was completely overgrown with tropical vines, in which little wrinkled, white beasties with long trunks tumbled about. Opening my eyes, I moved on.

Suddenly, a tree branch scratched my cheek. I took a few more steps and almost lost my balance because another tree branch hooked my coat. I realized that this was not accidental. It was the wood spirit trying to attract my attention to this place. I turned up the slope and, climbing a few yards, came across a beefy boletus prominently standing out above last year's fallen leaves. A bit further were two more, and just up the slope I came across a clearing full of field mushrooms. In only half an hour, I filled a large plastic bag to the top with mushrooms.

---

* We understand the "spirit of a particular region" to mean the full array of plants, animals, minerals, and bodies of water in that area.

Thoroughly soaked but satisfied, I descended the stony footpath. My bag of mushrooms felt pleasantly heavy in my hand. The sky had cleared, and millions of drops of water all around me sparkled in the sun. When at last I stumbled noisily into our apartment, Vasya had already come home from school. Seeing my bag of mushrooms, he frowned slightly but expressed his approval. A few minutes later he disappeared without a trace. He came back in the evening, when it was just growing dark. His plastic bucket and bag were overflowing with mushrooms. Vasya told me excitedly that in his enthusiasm he had got lost and ended up making a wide loop through the mountains.

After we established a friendly relationship with the spirit of the woods, our diet over the next three days consisted exclusively of mushroom dishes. Thick boletus soup bubbled in a large cast iron pot. Field mushrooms in sour cream stewed in our voluminous frying pan. Next to these enormous cooking pots sat a measly little pan in which two tiny potatoes were boiling. Our landlady, Vasilievna, stopped short at this sight, and, pointing at the little pan, enquired in amusement: "And what are you cooking here?"

We replied in unison: "Potatoes with mushrooms."

CLOUDS OVER SAINT PETERSBURG

It happened in autumn of 1995, in that glorious city on the Neva River—Saint Petersburg. Beard and Papa had arrived with the sacred mission of sowing magical seeds into the grateful hearts of the residents of this northern metropolis. Worn out by their virtuous and edifying labor, the two magicians were leisurely strolling along Nevsky Prospekt. The sky above them was covered over by a grey pall of clouds, but they greatly desired to behold the bright rays of the sun in the deep, blue sky. They raised up their voices to dear Vanya.

Beard spoke thus: "Most honorable Vanya! I offer to thee my sincerest gratitude for warning me that my fears could manifest—the clouds above may grow even thicker into threatening storm clouds, and torrential rains could burst forth causing the Neva River to flood over its banks and sweep us all away in its mighty current down to the Baltic Sea, where we would become food for the fishes. I offer to you a raccoon with silvery-blue fur raised up on its hind legs. In its front paws, it holds a silver child's bugle with a bright red pennant and yellow tassels, on which it plays the Soviet national anthem."

Papa proposed that they add sound to this picture and, with great inspiration, they sang out together as they walked along Nevsky Prospekt: "The unbreakable union of free republics…" Soon they turned toward the Church of the Savior on Spilled Blood,* and while they contemplated this edifice the sky gradually began to clear, and patches of blue sky appeared. But the sun was still hidden by clouds. Not far away they encountered street stalls filled with souvenirs—Russian nesting dolls, lacquer boxes, ornaments, military collectables, and all manner of knick-knacks from Soviet times. When the magicians had passed through these stalls, they noticed in the last one a silver child's bugle with a bright red pennant and yellow tassels, exactly like the one the raccoon was playing.

"Our gift to Vanya has materialized!" they exclaimed, bursting out laughing. At that moment, the last clouds covering the sun were dispersed, and irrepressible rays of sunlight surged down upon the earth. Papa and Beard rejoiced with all their hearts.

Remember that *we do not perform sorcery which alters the outer environment by force*. If manifesting sunny weather, as in the events described, would have in any way disturbed the natural balance, then the weather would have remained cloudy. Any magical act—in this case, thanksgiving—considers the interests of all participants in the game.

---

*The church built on the place where Czar Alexander II was murdered. [trans]

MISCELANEOUS STORIES

REGARDING INSECTS

Every spring, when the sun begins to grow hot, and the trees are clad in a mantle of white blossoms, our apartment is subject to the vicious attacks of mosquitoes. During the hot weather, we keep our balcony door wide open, and in the evening swarms of tiny vampires gather for the feast. As the night deepens, their humming inexorably increases. The winged warriors cover the walls and ceiling, and circle around everywhere. The most impatient among them dart down to their potential victims, despite the risk of being squashed. But the majority wait for that favorable hour, when the huge and awkward vessels of precious, red liquid finally go to bed. Each night, my wife and I experience excruciating torture. The mosquitoes constantly are buzzing around our ears, periodically piercing our flesh with their spiteful stings.

As soon as we begin to fall asleep, a loud smack drives away all sleep. Attempts to cover our heads with blankets are futile, because then we can't breath. Only one thought rankles our agitated brains: "When will our torment end?" The battle in the darkness continues until near dawn when, wholly exhausted, we finally fall asleep. In the morning, we get out of bed tired and listless, and spots of blood are spattered across our pillows.

We have tried every means of defense. Before going to sleep, I would go on the hunt with newspaper in hand to destroy the mosquitoes on the ceiling and walls. My wife would protest the mess I was making: "You should wipe them off with a rag, not smash them full force!" The aftermath of the slaughter would have to be whitewashed away, but, in the end, a new squadron instantly replaced all those I had annihilated.

We tried shutting the balcony door, barely tolerating the sweltering heat. However, even this was in vain, for as soon as we switched off the light, opened the door a crack, and climbed under the sheets, the insatiable aeronauts filled the space. My mother-in-law tried hanging a gauze curtain across the balcony doorway, but all the same the mosquitoes infiltrated through the weave of the cloth. We rubbed ourselves with a smelly Vietnamese ointment called "Golden Star," but it burned our skin like fire.

Having exhausted all other methods, I remembered my magical world view and performed a dance. During this dance, I had a vision of the Mosquito Queen in a low-cut gown. Pince-nez eyeglasses glistened on her serrated beak, and knitting needles flickered between her hairy legs. She was sitting on a bamboo throne, and at her side servants stood by in velvet livery, polishing her wings with a special elixir. The Queen looked very pleased. My dance finished with the mantra LABRIGOT.

That evening, when I went to bed, I once again heard the familiar humming. Doubts swirled through my mind: "Maybe it didn't work?" I comforted myself with the thought that perhaps the imperial decree of the Mosquito Queen hadn't yet reached the masses, so I repeated the mantra, imagining the Queen in all her finery. For the first couple of weeks, I didn't perceive any noticeable change. However, I had nothing else to fall back on, so I kept working with the mantra and image.

Eventually, sleep started coming sooner, and every night there were fewer and fewer mosquitoes. Finally, they disappeared altogether, except the occasional stray flitting in. All summer long we had virtually no mosquitoes, and ever since we have been under the protection of the Mosquito Queen. Sometimes, perhaps to test my vigilance, a lone kamikaze would dart in, but encountering my persistent LABRIGOT, he would fly away home or die a hero while fulfilling his call of duty.

Emboldened, I decided to grapple with the cockroaches, who had long ago thoroughly invaded our apartment. When entering the kitchen during the night, we would see throngs of the copper-colored parasites scuttling all over the table, the sink, and the floor. Some of the inveterate cockroaches were wholly unafraid of our presence and leisurely strolled about the room, ponderously dragging along their bloated bellies. Nothing had any effect on these brazen bugs—not cockroach traps, not egg yolks saturated with boric acid, not Chinese insecticidal chalk. Even the poisonous liquid my mother-in-law bought which would melt plastic failed to work.

I thanked the cockroach hordes for warning me that my greatest fears could manifest: they might multiply out of control until everything—clothes, dishes, food—would be covered over by cockroaches, and we would have to run away from our apartment to save ourselves.

I could not help but recall a poignant episode from my wild student days. One night, at about 4:00 am, I was awoken by compulsive banging on the door of my dormitory room. When I finally got up to open it, I found Dmitry—my close friend, classmate, and faithful drinking buddy—standing there distraught. He was shaking his balding head, appealing for mercy. Dmitry had been awakened by a terrible racket—a cockroach had crawled into his ear. Diving into my first-aid kit, I pulled out a disposable syringe and injected a substantial amount of water into my friend's ear. The little beast finally became still. In the morning, the doctor extracted a drowned cockroach from his ear.

After thanking the cockroach hordes, I offered them several ripe corn cobs stacked neatly together into a tipi. Kernels of corn were strewn about everywhere, and a plump bullfinch with a bright red breast was pecking them.

After that, whenever I saw a cockroach, I would watch my imaginary movie *The Fledgling of the Corn*. Actually, I stopped even caring about the cockroaches, paying little attention to them, so I hardly noticed that they were decreasing. One day, I simply realized that I hadn't seen any for a while. Just in case, I asked my wife about it, and she confirmed that the cockroaches had gone.

For about a year, they didn't visit our home at all. After that, there were occasional, somewhat timid raids on our living quarters, and I would renew my work with the corn cob tipi and the plump bullfinch. Now there are no cockroaches at all in our apartment.

This summer, an announcement appeared in the entryway to our building: "At the request of residents, fumigation against cockroaches will take place in this building in the near future. This work will be carried out for a fee for those who want it. We recommend that all participate in this project to prevent the migration of insects into neighboring apartments. Citizens! We can exterminate the cockroaches through our united efforts!"

After reading these words written by some unknown genius, I remembered my bullfinch, and not a single immigrant was discovered on our territory.

Here is a similar story told by Papa:

Several years ago we were being tormented by mosquitoes. It was winter and the temperature outside was below zero, but we couldn't get any sleep due to the mosquitoes. Each evening I would hunt them down with our vacuum cleaner, but to no avail. During the night they would infiltrate back into our apartment. If we woke up in the middle of the night, it was difficult to fall back asleep—the annoying hum of mosquitoes wouldn't allow it. We could even hear them under the blankets. In the morning, it was impossible to practice yoga. As soon as I settled into a posture, an attack squadron would dart down toward me. In the end, my patience gave out, and I remembered my magic.

"Thank you, most honored mosquitoes, for warning me that I could be doomed until the end of my days to sleeping each night with your relentless shrill singing in my ears." After this, I dedicated a dance to the mosquitoes, and they quickly disappeared.

However, this story has a sequel. I live on the ground floor. In the building basement, there were several large, rank puddles, because the plumbers would drain water from the central heating system straight onto the basement floor. I asked a plumber I knew whether it was possible to do anything to get rid of these puddles. He answered that nothing could be done—a serious error had been made when they built the building.

Six months later, my kitchen faucet started leaking, and I called a plumber. He came very late in the evening, because he had been down in the basement changing the pipes. While he was repairing my faucet, I asked out of curiosity how they managed to work in the cellar with all those huge puddles around. The plumber replied that the puddles were gone. He had cleaned out the clogged drain.

That's how, while working with the mosquitoes multiplying in those puddles, I was simultaneously working on the puddles themselves, without even being aware of it. Such occurrences often happen in the practice of magic.

BEET LOVERS IN RYABINOVKA

There is a village of summerhouses not far from Moscow called Ryabinovka. It has always been famous for its extraordinary harvests of beets, carrots, cucumbers, and other vegetables, but one year misfortune struck—the gardens were invaded by armies of grey mice. The local fruit and vegetable growers asked Anna to turn to magicians for help. Anna worked with my wife and had more than once referred clients to me. So I wasn't surprised when she asked me yet again: "Will you perform some magic for me?"

It turned out that this wasn't the first year the mice had "helped" Anna with her harvest. The previous summer the insidious rodents had multiplied out of control, devastating her "plantation." They especially had a taste for Anna's beets, and almost the entire harvest of this sweet root crop was devoured by the mice. Carrots, too, had suffered huge losses, nor did the mice disdain the cucumbers. The garden beds were riddled with tunnels, and there were holes everywhere.

Anna had tried every known method to battle them. She had managed to get the latest, imported pesticide from the Horticulture Institute, but the smelly compound proved too weak for the mice of Ryabinovka. Stuffing camphor balls down into the mouse catacombs also didn't work. All the local gardeners were in the same situation. Finally, at the start of the coming growing season, Anna decided to resort to the help of magicians.

"Maybe I could make some kind of deal with the Mouse King," I thought. The Mouse King had a respectable appearance—a shiny, bald head, curled up whiskers, and a huge belly which dragged along the ground as he walked. A Pavel Bure watch on a thick gold chain peeped out from his vest pocket. Puffing and panting, the king could barely move his legs. For a gift, I offered him a large wheelbarrow, and straightaway he loaded his belly into it, rolling it along in front of him with dignity. However, something was still missing—a certain flair, the icing on the cake. At that point, His Royal Highness began to hum the latest hit song: "Tell me, tell me what you need, what you need. So I may give you, I may give you what you want…" I realized right then that negotiations at the highest level had been successfully accomplished. I described to Anna the appearance of the Mouse King and instructed her to concentrate on this image while humming the simple melody.

During the hot days of summer, I met Anna again. She was quick to boast that the mice had disappeared completely. Her garden was in complete order, and she was expecting an overabundance of vegetables. A menacing sentry had appeared in her garden. Several times Anna had seen among the beets a large, thick grass snake leisurely basking in the sun. What's more, the mice had evacuated the entire village, and the workers in the fields and gardens of Ryabinovka were able to breathe easily at last. That year Anna was blessed with a bounteous harvest. One day in the fall, she showed up at our apartment with a huge sack of select, sugary beets for us to enjoy through the winter.

THE CRIMSON-COLORED
SPORTS COAT

One cold March night, a pretty young woman named Marina came to our door. She was obviously very upset by something. The situation which Marina found herself in seemed utterly hopeless to her, yet she was looking for a miracle. Somewhat confused, she hurriedly began her grievous tale.

I work as a bookkeeper for a certain firm. The director (I'll call him Borisovich) is constantly criticizing me, literally for any and every reason. He used to be a KGB officer and brought to his new position the style and spirit of his previous work. If I am away from my desk for just five minutes, the director would be waiting to abuse and chastise me: "Where have you been off to? Is this your work or some kind of girls' gossip circle? Young people are so spoiled these days. Too bad it's not like the old days. Then you'd learn to do as you're told!"

When several of us show up late for work at the same time, he always singles me out. If I'm out on my lunch break, Borisovich is sure to be looking for me to do something—to go to the bank, or pay some bill, or whatever. Once I came back from an errand for him and was ten minutes late. I was carrying a large handbag. Borisovich was beside himself, shouting that I had been out shopping all over town.

So basically I'm terrified of him. Everything goes wrong whenever we talk to each other, and my work is suffering because of it. I bend over backwards to do my job well, but all I get back is blame and disapproval. It's true that Borisovich criticizes everyone, but no one as much as me. The director uses me to "fill in the gaps" when there's no one else, and now he's planning to send me on a business trip to Uriupinsk, even though I still don't understand the company business that well.

At home I sit in terror that tomorrow will be just the same. My knees tremble at the thought that Borisovich will yell at me again.

Marina gave thanks to her boss, because he was warning her by his actions about the troubles which could befall her if she didn't change her attitude toward the situation. For example, the following developments could easily occur: due to the incessant trembling of her knees, she could develop a bouncing gait as she walks, like Charlie Chaplin; because of her constant fear, she could wind up in a psycho ward; and to deal with her excessive outbursts of tears, she might have to always carry around a whole suitcase full of handkerchiefs. After this "optimistic" monologue, our heroine felt much better.

I suggested to Marina that she remember a time when the director was in a good mood and shared that with the people around him. Then she could affirm this new quality in him by giving him a new name. Magicians call this renaming strategy searching for the ray of light.

It proved quite difficult for Marina to recall an actual event when Borisovich generously shared happiness with others. Like a colored lens which allows only rays of a certain color to pass through, she had formed an image of her boss as a gloomy and aggressive person. She had to search deep into her memory. At last Marina remembered a time when Borisovich had acted like a true gentleman, and she instantly lit up with a wide smile.

The director usually wore "gloomy-colored" clothes—black or grey suits and turtlenecks—and his mood was just as gloomy. But one time Borisovich came to work dressed in a crimson-colored sports coat. As Marina put it: "The sports coat really suited him well. I noticed that the director, too, liked his unusual outfit very much; it made him feel extremely gracious." The most amazing thing was that the boss's mood was festive as well. He simply radiated joy. When Borisovich entered the room where Marina was sitting with her co-workers, he greeted them with a friendly smile and complimented each of them in turn. For several moments afterwards, a deathly silence permeated the room. Nobody could believe his behavior!

There could be no doubt—this was the ray of light she had been looking for. His new name was obvious: *"I am the one who gives compliments in a crimson-colored sports coat."* Marina preferred the shortened name: *"I am the one in the crimson-colored sports coat."* From that point on, she repeated this name whenever circumstances required, trying to fan to life that tiny spark of light she had found.

Here is Marina's narration about the further events of this story.

I repeated the magical formula every morning while going to work. If Borisovich criticized me, or if he seemed about to start, I affirmed him as *"the one in the crimson-colored sports coat."* It was obvious that the director liked this very much. He would immediately stop being aggressive and calm down. Once I went into his office to get some papers signed, repeating to myself the phrase about the crimson-colored sports coat, and I could tell that Borisovich instantly felt it. Previously, he either would have yelled at me, or signed them without lifting his head. But this time he looked up, smiled, and asked: "How are you doing? Do you feel well? Is everything OK here at work? Is anyone bothering you?" I had never heard anything like this from him before. Since that time, our relationship improved day by day. Before long, I stopped being afraid of the director. My co-workers also noticed that Borisovich had become kinder and more friendly with them.

However, Marina didn't manage to get out of the business trip to Uriupinsk, where the head office of the company was located. Her boss told her: "You just have to show up, drop off the papers, and come back." But in reality the trip promised to be very difficult. Marina knew that the financial report for the head office had been done sloppily with many mistakes. There was little chance of getting away so easily. Besides, in Uriupinsk nobody had been assigned to take responsibility for receiving these documents. In other words, there was no one there expecting to review the report. Marina was the youngest in the bookkeeping department. Therefore the "honor" of the Uriupinsk mission had fallen on her. Her anxiety that she would be passed from one person to the next and the trip would be a total failure were fully justified. Marina asked me to help her work with this issue.

I performed a dance which finished with a graceful sweep of my arm and a mantra which would be nearly impossible to write down on paper. This mantra was more like an indecent sound, as if somebody had let loose a loud fart. "Armed" with this mantra, Marina departed for Uriupinsk.

You can imagine Marina's surprise when she saw a brand new Mercedes waiting for her at the Uriupinsk airport, and it belonged to not just anyone but to the head bookkeeper for the firm! Every morning, this "modest" car picked up Marina at her hotel and delivered her back in the evening (she had to work very late). Marina was lodged in a luxurious room in the best hotel in the city, and each morning an elaborate breakfast awaited her in the restaurant.

Again we will give Marina the floor:

It was the first time that I'd performed such responsible work. The report was extremely complicated and at first nothing made sense. The chief bookkeeper from Uriupinsk reminded me very much of Borisovich before his renaming. Every day she yelled at everyone, scolding them constantly. This "company dragon" was with me constantly until 9:00 or 10:00 in the evening, helping me rewrite the report. I never stopped repeating my mantra. Nadezhda Alexeevna, of course, criticized me but also showed a certain sympathy—she pointed out errors and patiently explained what wasn't clear. She also talked about when she was young, saying that she had similar difficulties.

Everyone around us was amazed: "What's happened to Alexeevna? Why has she taken such a liking to this girl?" All my anxiety that no one would deal with me, that they would reject the report and send me back, or even fire me, was for naught. The report was accepted. They bought me a ticket home, and even treated me to a farewell party in one of the fanciest restaurants in town.

When he heard the outcome of my trip, Borisovich was in ecstasy and immediately went to the general manager, asking him to promote me to the recently vacated position of head bookkeeper. The general manager objected: "That's all very well and good, but it seems a little early for her to be trusted with such a responsible position. She's a young woman, and nobody knows what she might be up to." The "crimson-colored sports coat" passionately stood up for me (he had never done anything like this before).

He said that he had worked with me for two years, that he knew me well, and, in his opinion, I was a reliable person perfectly suited to this job. The general manager gave in and signed my appointment as head bookkeeper. Incidentally, Alexeevna recommended me as well.

Two years have passed since the events described above. Marina has had to visit Uriupinsk several times since, and the formidable bookkeeper there considers her one of the best employees of the firm. We can only add that Marina was also very pleased with her subsequent relationship to Borisovich, and when the "crimson-colored sports coat" moved to another company, he proclaimed that he would be glad if she ever decided to work for him there. Recently for International Women's Day, he called his former office to congratulate all the women working there, and noted Marina specifically.

BEFRIENDING A MENACING
SECURITY GUARD

The events described below took place in the village of Nekra-sovka (cf. Tale of the Little Buddha). For some time I had regularly been going to the local hospital. At the entrance, the security guard in his trim black uniform would quickly glance at my temporary pass as I confidently walked through the gates to the hospital.

Once, though, I was stopped by a young fellow with an inscrutable expression on his face. He took my pass, carefully examined the signature and stamp, and held it up to the light. Then he opened up some kind of logbook—probably a registry of temporary passes—and leafed through its pages for several minutes. My name wasn't there. The security guard looked at me suspiciously and shot out a volley of questions:

"Who are you? What is the purpose of your visit? Where are you going, and who are you visiting? Who gave you this pass? And why does it expire in three days?"

Attempting to maintain an unperturbed expression, I responded that I was a doctor, and that I was going to a particular ward to work with a patient with a rare condition that was of exceptional interest to the scientific world. My answers didn't satisfy this zealous law enforcement officer, and with a facial expression which promised nothing good for me, he lifted the telephone receiver.

While waiting for his superior officer to come, I uttered inwardly a thanksgiving monologue. The security guard was warning me by his actions that the doors to all public places could become closed to me. I barely had time to finish paint- ing the image of my gift when a severe old lady in horn- rimmed glasses appeared in the doorway. The security guard leaped to his feet, handed her my pass, and reported his sus- picions.

His superior turned out to be impetuous and talkative to the extreme. She drew me aside and, wildly gesticulating, started lecturing me about current events in her loud, discor- dant voice. She told me how "the mafia is spreading its tenta- cles into every corner of the country, increasing the possibility of terrorist attacks. And in these troublesome times, certain irresponsible elements are trying to fraudulently infiltrate the hospital grounds."

"I need to rename this lady, and quick," I thought. "Or it'll be the end of me." She kept talking non-stop, without letting me get a single word in.

Suddenly, the ray of light was revealed to me within her frenzied monologue: "Despite the complex political, eco- nomic, and social situation in Russia today, the duty I have been entrusted with to protect this hospital requires me to be always on combat alert. Not even animals or birds shall pass these gates unnoticed. The defense of the borders of this institution is in secure hands."

That was it! Her name was clear: *"I am the one who vigi- lantly stands ready on combat alert."*

The severe old lady continued to describe the efficient or- ganization of the security service, and I nodded my head with understanding, repeating the name I had found. With relief I noticed that the volume and tone of her voice was softening considerably. There was a short pause, and I expressed my admiration of how well the security of the hospital had been effected. With these words, I affirmed in the commanding officer her new name.

Our conversation became more equitable, and even a mutual affinity rose up between us. The incident was forgotten, and we parted almost as friends. Having run out of steam, the security officer-in-charge remembered her other pressing duties, handed back my pass, and briskly marched off to perform another urgent task in her relentless fight against crime. I walked through the hospital grounds, rustling the fallen leaves and quietly singing: "Our service is both dangerous and tough..."* Needless to say, after this meeting I was able to enter the hospital freely and without delay.

* A line from the theme song of a Soviet police television series. [trans]

WORKSHOP IN ARKHANGELSK

Sergey sought me out, as he was interested in the school for magicians. He introduced himself as the director of a jogging club in Arkhangelsk called "Catch Me If You Can." Recently, Sergey was not only organizing marathon races, but he had also founded a spiritual club. The premises of "Catch Me If You Can" had been refurbished and a small store was opened where Sergey sold books, incense, beads, audio and video cassettes—the typical items you find in such shops. In addition, Sergey organized seminars and training workshops, inviting leaders from all over Russia. Or members could just drop in on their days off to meet with friends and discuss various lofty topics over tea.

Sergey invited me to lead a four-day training session in magic. Previous to this, I had never led a workshop for so many days, although I had conducted seminars at two recent gatherings—north of St. Petersburg and on the Yakhroma River near Moscow. Also, for several months I had been leading a magician's group in Moscow.

It took about 24 hours by train to reach Arkhangelsk. On the way, I wrote out a brief outline for the first day of the seminar. At the appointed hour, I arrived at the Cultural Center where the workshop was to be held. The meeting hall was palatial—with varnished parquet floor, carpet runners, a piano, and plush chairs. To my surprise, a lot of people came. Only in such a provincial town could a young man, unknown to anyone, gather such a large audience. I started losing my nerve and faltered as I spoke, stumbling on my words while constantly staring down at my notes. Finally, a glowering woman who looked like an owl, unable to take it any more, announced indignantly that she hadn't come there to listen to someone just read through his notes. I blushed and stopped looking down at my outline.

After that the "owl," whose name was Nina, blatantly provoked me several times, clearly trying to disrupt the seminar. At one point, while she was preaching about the proper way to lead a seminar, I pictured Nina at a resort up in the mountains. Several wooden cottages dotted a high ridge at tree line. The sun was shining brightly, reflected in a million tiny snowflakes. Nina was sitting at a table in an open-air café, enjoying a cup of aromatic coffee while basking in the warm sun. Everything became clear: *"I am the one who serves Nina a cup of coffee in the mountains."*

An inspired idea flashed through my mind like lightning— the time had come to present some games and meditations. It is always interesting to observe how in these games adult men and women gradually transform into children. In fact, if only one of them is liberated, the others, watching him, also begin to relax. Finally, excitement sparkled in Nina's eyes and she smiled. With the games, I was able to successfully finish up the first day of the seminar.

I thanked Vanya for warning me that, if I lack self-confidence, I could be pelted with rotten cabbages and, like that great scam artist Ostap Bender, end up having to run away desperately from an angry mob. I offered Vanya a purple Klein bottle, one-third full of a mercury-colored liquid. A mother-of-pearl ellipse surrounded by a light pink halo slowly pulsated above it.

Nina didn't come for the second day of the seminar. Evidently, she was satisfied with coffee in the mountains. I was definitely feeling more at ease, and our group work proceeded calmly and fruitfully. It became apparent that I had mastered magical techniques sufficiently well, and I no longer needed my notes. I explained the fundamentals of thanksgiving and renaming, and toward the end of the seminar some of the participants were already telling me about their successes. On the last day, I led a very beautiful meditation which people in Arkhangelsk remember even to this day. The seminar concluded successfully. Afterwards, Sergey presented me with a gift of a wooden "bird of happiness" as well as a small honorarium, and I headed homeward.

That summer at a gathering near St. Petersburg, Beard and I gave talks about magic for four days to an audience of about fifty people. The conditions were very inspiring for this work. The entire camp was enraptured by the games. Everywhere you could hear: "Thank you Vanya…" and "I give to you…" and "I am the one who…" At this point, though, I should say a few words about Vasya.

On the first day of camp, as I was on my way to the river for a swim, I suddenly heard a child shout loudly: "Look, there's the magician over there!" ("The magician" is what many people call me at these gatherings). It was Vasya, a blond boy of about six.

I had first met him at a previous gathering. I was leading a seminar focused on giving thanks, and it turned out that Vasya was listening. Apparently, he had been playing nearby, and his sensitive child's mind had naturally absorbed the incoming information. Toward the end of the gathering, his mother, Tanya, came up to me with a letter. The boy had written a message addressed to the "Chief Magician," in which he asked for a balloon. There were many foreigners at that gathering. A German woman, Kony, had given all the children beautiful balloons, but Vasya somehow managed to pop his balloon right away. He gave thanks to Vanya, but just to be sure he wrote a letter to the Chief Magician. Needless to say, while Vasya was sleeping, Tanya had placed two balloons by his side. Now you can understand Vasya's reaction when he saw me at that next gathering.

We dashed toward each other, and I swept him up into my arms. We talked for a long time about our lives. Later Tanya told me secretly that Vasya had been teaching magic to the children in his kindergarten.

One evening, some of us were sitting on logs around a campfire sharing our dreams. Natasha was saying that from time to time she has nightmares with vivid scenes of sexual violence. Beard and I agreed to help her sort out the issue underlying these dreams. We first asked her to tell us about her relationships with men, and she began to recall episodes from her personal history. At that very moment, Vasya passed by us. A tambourine was stuck under his Panama hat, and he was playing it as he walked. When he caught sight of me, he exclaimed: *"I am the one who plays the tambourine."* I asked Vasya if we could borrow his instrument and suggested to Natasha that she put it under her hat. She walked around in a circle repeating: *"I am the one who plays the tambourine."*

While Natasha was doing this, Vasya amazed us yet again. He came up to me and said: "Look what I've got." Taking off his sandals, he showed me several small pine needles inside. These also were given to Natasha. She put them into her gym shoes and continued playing the tambourine. But Vasya had already come up with yet another new innovation: "Do you want to see what else I've got?" He stretched out the elastic of his underwear. Inside, a few short, stubby sticks were revealed. Everyone burst into laughter as the sticks were ceremoniously handed over to Natasha with appropriate instructions.

The following year we met Natasha again. The nightmares had not only left her, but her personal life had also greatly improved.

During that summer, I gained more confidence and experience in leading seminars, so when Sergey again invited me to Arkhangelsk, there was no doubt of success.

I arrived in Arkhangelsk in the morning. The seminar was to begin at 6 pm, so I had the whole day to prepare. After working for about two hours, I started feeling hungry. I stepped into the kitchen, turned on the tea kettle, and noticed a plastic bag of dried apricots. I tried to untie the bag, but wasn't having any luck—the knot was tied too tightly. My hand automatically grabbed for a knife. Evidently, the impulse instilled in humanity by Alexander the Great was at work. Wait! Literally a few minutes ago, I had been mentally playing through the beginning of the seminar. I could still hear resounding in my mind: "Everything is a part of myself." Why should I bring more unnecessary violence into the world by cutting off the bag's "head"! I decided to work on the knot, and then to use this as an example in the seminar.

"I thank you, dear knot, for warning me that you could stay tied tight despite all my efforts, and that many such tangled knots and situations could appear in my life—my bootlaces could become so tangled that I would have to spend the rest of my life without ever being able to take off my boots, even at night. I would have to bathe in them, and then they would be all squishy and would squelch as I walked. Because you have warned me about this, most honored knot, I offer you thanks from the depths of my heart."

In order to rename myself, I first imagined myself as a knot; I became the knot. I could feel my body tightening up, which told me that I needed to relax. A massage might do the trick!

I gently caressed the knot.* My new name was revealed: *"I am the one who massages the knot."* Next, I tried pulling gently at the tangled part of the knot from different angles until I could feel it gradually coming undone.

After treating myself to herbal tea with sweet-scented honey and dried apricots, I again sat down to prepare for the seminar, jotting down notes as needed. Suddenly, my ball-point pen stopped writing. Since I was already riding a wave of thanksgiving, my new name came to me instantly: *"I am the one who warms the pen with the heat of my hand."* The pen began writing smoothly and evenly.

I used these two simple metaphors during the seminar to illustrate the idea of renaming.

On the first day of the training, I received an impressive support signal. I had felt that my first seminar in Arkhangelsk had been weak. Nonetheless, it became clear that many participants at that seminar had managed to resolve some very complex problems: some had received apartments, others had significantly increased their income, and still others had improved relations with their families. Several "newly-minted" magicians had also helped their friends successfully resolve various issues.

The following day also began auspiciously. On the previous evening, Mitya had approached me with an issue—his wife was obsessed with jealousy. Mitya came up with this image for her: *"I am the one who shoots balloons with a crossbow."*

Returning home quite late, Mitya was surprised to find his wife fast asleep. Previously, she had always waited up for her husband to find out where on earth he'd been. Dinner was on

---

* It's interesting that, while typing this phrase into the computer, I am listening to the group *Enigma*, and keep hearing the word "relax," followed by "take a deep rest."

the stove, so our hero had a bite to eat and went to bed. Upon waking the next morning, he hunkered down under the covers as always, listening intently. Instead of the expected complaints and threats, he heard his wife singing lightheartedly in the kitchen as she washed the dishes. Apparently, she was in a great mood. What's more, this happened even though Mitya had completely forgotten that he had renamed his wife, and he had not repeated her new name that morning even once.

On my next visit to Arkhangelsk, I learned that Mitya no longer had any problems with his wife being jealous.

I will finish this narration with one last edifying story (although I could go on forever). When I explained the technique of renaming by searching for the root, Tamara came forward with her problem. She had deposited her life savings (a good amount of money) into a bank which suddenly cut off all withdrawals. In fact, it turned out that several participants at the seminar also had deposited money into this same bank.

To begin, Tamara thanked the bank for warning her that she could lose all her money. Then I asked her when she had faced similar situations in her life. It turned out that her children had borrowed money from her to buy furniture and never paid her back. Then Tamara remembered that she herself had not repaid a debt to her mother. In the end, she realized that she owed her mother attention and emotional comfort. For the last five years of her life, her mother had been very weak, and Tamara stopped taking her to her summerhouse—she would have had to spend too much time caring for her instead of working in the garden. Her mother was very disappointed by this because she loved spending her summers in the country.

Tamara imagined that she was taking her to the summerhouse. She visualized this picture: her mother is sitting on the porch basking in the sun, and Tamara brings her a basket of freshly picked strawberries. Her mother eats the strawberries with pleasure, and a grateful smile spreads across her face.

Tamara felt a heavy weight which had long burdened her soul simply fall away. Her joy was so great, she couldn't hold back her tears. Flushed and happy, she walked around the circle, repeating: *"I am the one who serves strawberries to my mom,"* and in unison the entire group affirmed this name back to her.

Soon afterwards, I heard the end to this story. In less than a month, the bank began allowing withdrawals. It had established a maximum amount for each client, but Tamara managed to get twice that in cash, and the rest was compensated in the form of a Russian jeep and a garage. The bank still owed her a little money, but it intended to continue paying off its debts.

A MAGICAL TRANSFIGURATION

I work as a clerk in a shop which has two owners. One of them, Alexey Alexandrovich, often used to stop into the shop to reproach us in his horrible, offensive voice. "What kind of joint are you running here? Look at this mess! The price tags are cockeyed, and the displays are all wrong."

His endless nagging—not only of me, but of everyone else as well—put us in a terrible mood, and we would just quit trying: the cashier would make mistakes, and the young clerks would scurry off into the far-off corners of the shop to hide, trying in any way to avoid Alexey.

Alexey had three children, and apparently he used to constantly berate his wife and children, forcing them to sit in a corner when they misbehaved. And this practice extended to his underlings as well—he tried to put us, too, "in the corner." Alexey's outer appearance did not correspond to his position—his shoelaces were always untied, his running shoes worn out, his hair stuck out in every direction, his hands always grimy with machine oil, and on his lip was some sort of scar or sore.

I decided to apply the technique of renaming the actual obstacle. I mentally bathed Alexey, gave him a massage, and cut his hair; then I thought about what to do with the sore on his lip. I imagined an old man from Tibet handing him a healing balm made from herbs gathered high in the mountains. I tenderly daubed the fragrant balm onto his sore. It was very gentle and instantly absorbed into the skin, which became smooth and elastic. My name became: *"I am the one who heals the wound with an herbal balm from Tibet."* I walked around the circle repeating this name and looked deep into the eyes of each person in the group, seeking affirmation of the healing name.

For quite a while after his renaming, Alexey stopped dropping by the shop. He didn't even come when our shop moved to a new location. Finally, after four months Alexey visited us. At first I didn't recognize him. He looked like a model off the cover of a Western magazine—a fashionable haircut, smooth skin, and a formal suit and tie. You could almost fall in love with him. The sore on his lip was hardly noticeable; you could see it only if you looked very carefully. He spoke in a calm, even voice: "Ladies and gentlemen, you need something here to inspire you. Perhaps some flowers." Since then, Alexey—as if reborn—has become kind and even-tempered, and if ever he criticizes anyone, it is usually for good cause.

Our shop specializes in outdoor wear. The premises of the shop are small, so our storeroom is located in the cellar. The rats grew fond of this cellar and with great satisfaction treated themselves not only to the cardboard boxes but also to the clothing. The stockroom workers complained that the emboldened rats weren't in the least afraid of humans. They scurried around under their feet and hampered their work. Some of them finally bought guns, and whenever they had a spare moment they descended the stairs to hunt the rodents. But the number of grey predators never seemed to decrease.

Once I went down to the cellar and froze in my tracks—a rat the size of a good-sized kitten was sitting right there on the computer keyboard. Unperturbed, it took no notice of me at all and continued on with its business. Obviously, it considered this its lawful territory.

Another time, I saw five rats sitting in a line on the staircase leading down to the cellar. It seemed that they were looking at me with hope glistening in their eyes. I must confess that I took pity on the poor, hungry rats and decided to secretly feed them some bread. Let them eat more than just cardboard and cloth!

Numerous attempts to poison the rats were unsuccessful, and finally I decided that it was time to utilize magical techniques. I came up with the mantra TURIMEKS which I repeated constantly. In the end, the rat conundrum was resolved quite unexpectedly—six months later our firm purchased new premises and the shop was moved.

THE LATE NIGHT EXPRESS

A magician's relationship with public transportation often develops most auspiciously—they rarely get stranded at stations or delayed by lines or traffic jams.

Late one night in the spring, I was on my way home. Coming out of the Tsaritsyno subway station, my heart sank to see only a few lonely figures milling around the bus stop. It was nearly midnight, and past experience told me that I was facing a long wait for the bus. A chilly breeze ruffled my hair and beard. I had only one hope—magic.

The skeptic in me called out desperately: "How can magic help me here? What bus could possibly pass by at this time of night? Or do you expect a helicopter to just swoop down and pick you up?"

But the magician in me held firm, and I started up my usual line: "Thank you, dear Vanya, for warning me that my current world view could prove true—I will be stuck here for God knows how long waiting for the bus and, chilled to the bone, finally be forced to hoof it home on foot. I offer you a horseman in a flowing cloak, galloping headlong over the hills of the grassy steppe.

The skeptic continued to whine something about sophomoric wisdom: "No matter how hard you try, dude, in the end you'll just get... an 'F.'" But the horseman kept galloping impetuously over the silvery hills. This internal dialogue lasted no more than three minutes, and then a miracle occurred!

A handsome Mercedes bus came rolling around the corner. The sign posted on its windshield said "Express Bus: Tsarit-syno Subway Station—Platform Biriulevo." I had never before seen an express bus on this route, and at that time Mercedes buses were quite rare on the streets of Moscow. It's no wonder that I was so surprised by it all. My first thought was: "Is this a dream?"

As I sat in the warm, cozy passenger compartment, smoothly and soundlessly gliding along the dark streets, I had time to contemplate the utter unpredictability of this amazing world we live in.

AFTERWORD

"If all fixed beliefs are illusions, then even your proposition that all fixed beliefs are illusions is also an illusion."

"That is absolutely true."

"Then what can one believe in?"

"Exactly."

Luke Rhinehart—Transformation

Any theory professing some degree of universality is a myth.

Ernest Tsvetkov—Psychonomics
or the Programmable Mind

Never expect someone else to show you the way or to make you happy.

Richard Bach—Running From Safety

"It is no longer up to you whether to go or not, my dear. You are a myth, a legend; and rumor ascribes to you great deeds."

"Rumor doesn't come up with such foolishness."

"I can't believe that!"

"Yes, Mr. Ramkopf, I demand that you withdraw this ridiculous book."

From the film Münchhausen Himself

We expect that, after reading this book, many readers will immediately begin practicing magical techniques, and we're certain that they will succeed.

If you wish to schedule a training session in your city, please contact us by email at: *g_u_rangov@mail.ru* or *d_o_lohov@aport.ru*; our webpage is *www.simoron.ru*.

You can obtain excellent training online by participating in the Magicians Symposium at *http://www.simoron.ru/phpBB3/*. Also, in the newsletter "Magical Fireworks" you can find news from magician's conferences, material from seminars, and magical stories. To subscribe, go online to *http://subscribe.ru/catalog/psychology.wizards*.*

The authors *do not maintain an office to receive clients*; however, anyone who wishes to attain mastery in magic can attend their seminars. The authors *do not answer letters* requesting mantras, renaming, etc., but rather encourage the reader *to be creative* and take the initiative to deal with their issues themselves. In order to learn something, you must first have the intention to learn it—i.e., you must start *doing work on your own*. Whoever *attempts* to become a magician surely *becomes* one. "Whether you succeed or not, *just do something, anything*! Don't sit on your hands waiting for someone else to solve your problems."

To be a magician, all you have to do is try applying the techniques in various sequences at every opportunity, carefully cultivating *your personal power*. People often write that small issues are nearly always resolved easily, but with the big ones—nothing. We believe that it is best not to distinguish

* The online resources cited here are in the Russian language. [trans]

between important and secondary goals. Don't be upset if you do not get the results you expect, but be encouraged by your achievements, attributing to yourself in advance ever higher standing as a magician. If something does not resolve itself over a long period of time, and you have persistently worked with it creatively, then something unexpected will surely happen instead: if not money, then love; if not love, then health; if not health, then money.

Sometimes we get the question: "I did everything written in the book but still nothing happened. What did I do wrong?"

Keep faith! And remember: *"Everything that I do, I do in the best possible way."*

Many other letters ask: "Which particular technique should I use to resolve an issue?" or "Which technique is the most powerful?" We would respond by stressing that the key element is to remember that *you are a magician* (i.e., you have the power to alter your world), so it's really not relevant which specific technique you use—giving thanks to the obstacle, renaming yourself, or performing a magical dance. It's not the particular technique which is important, but rather the creative impulse behind it, the flight of your imagination—when your eyes are ablaze with light and you experience that sensuous warmth glowing within your heart, that moment when you feel on the verge of taking off into space...

We hope that you will *play* with magic, discovering the joy of practicing magic which is so well expressed in this song of Ostap Bender:

> I do not weep, I do not cry.
> Just ask me, friend, I will not lie.
> All life's a game, and who's to blame?
> I love this life, I'm glad I came!

Why should I apologize?
They just submit, why agonize?
Surely skill and joyous glee
By right must charge a modest fee.

You must agree that such allure—
To hit the mark although obscure,
My eagle-eye, my hustle—and
Forbidden fruit drops in my hand.

What joy to slip along the edge!
Be still, my angels—don't dismay!
Please do not judge me for my sins,
But see how beautifully I play!

RECOMMENDED READING

Russian Folk Tales.

Bach, Richard. *Illusions* (1977). *Running from Safety* (1994).
Bandler, Richard. *Using Your Brain for a Change* (1985).
Brown, Joseph Epes. *The Sacred Pipe* (1953).
Carroll, Lewis. *Alice's Adventures in Wonderland* (1865). *Through the Looking Glass* (1871).
Castaneda, Carlos. *The Teachings of Don Juan* (1968). *A Separate Reality* (1971). *Journey to Ixtlan* (1972). *Tales of Power* (1974). *The Second Ring of Power* (1977). *The Eagle's Gift* (1981). *The Fire From Within* (1984). *The Power of Silence* (1987). *The Art of Dreaming* (1993).
Chopra, Deepak. *The Way of the Wizard* (1995).
Coelho, Paulo. *The Alchemist* (1988). *The Fifth Mountain* (1996). *Veronica Decides to Die* (1998). *The Devil and Miss Prym* (2000).
Donner, Florinda. *Being-in-Dreaming* (1991).
Fry, Max. *Nest of the Chimera. My Ragnarok* (1998).
Garfield, Patricia. *Creative Dreaming* (1974).
Harner, Michael. *The Way of the Shaman* (1980).
Heinlein, Robert. *Stranger in a Strange Land* (1961).
King, Serge. *Urban Shaman* (1990).
Kliuev, Evgeny. *Between Two Chairs* (1988). *Book of Ghosts* (2001).
Koval, Yuri. *The Lightest Boat in the World* (1984). *Syer-Vyer* (1998).

LaBerge, Stephen. *Lucid Dreaming* (1985). *Lucid Dreaming: A Concise Guide to Awakening in Your Dreams and in Your Life* (2004).

Le Guin, Ursula. *A Wizard of Earthsea* (1968).

Lukyanenko, Sergey. *Labyrinth of Reflections* (1997). *False Mirrors* (1999).

Monroe, Robert. *Journeys out of the Body* (1971). *Far Journeys* (1992). *Ultimate Journey* (1994).

Neihardt, John. *Black Elk Speaks* (1932).

Nosov, Nikolay. *The Adventures of Neznaika and His Friends* (1953). *Neznaika in Sun City* (1958).

Ouspensky, Petr. *In Search of the Miraculous* (1949).

Pelevin, Victor. *Chapaev and Emptiness* (1996). *The Life of Insects* (1993). *The Yellow Arrow* (1993). *Generation "P"* (1999).

Rhinehart, Luke. *Transformation* (1997).

Solo, Vseslav. *Fundamentals of Magic* (1994). *The Temple Gates* (1994).

Strugatsky, Arkady and Boris. *Monday Starts on Saturday* (1965).

Tolkien, J. R. R. *Leaf by Niggle and Other Magical Tales* (1945).

Tsvetkov, Ernest. *Master of Self-Knowledge or Immersion into "I"* (1995). *Psychonomics or the Programmable Mind* (1999).

Volkov, Alexander. *The Wizard of the Emerald City* (1939).

Yogananda, Paramahansa. *Autobiography of a Yogi* (1946).

Zelazny, Roger. *The Chronicles of Amber 1-10* (1970-1991).

GLOSSARY OF RUSSIAN PERSONAL NAMES

Feminine

(diminutive forms *italicized*)

Alexandra
Alexeevna (patronymic)
Alla
Anya (Anna)
Darya
Dundusa
Elena (*Lena, Lenulia*)
Frosia (Efrosinya)
Galya (Galina)
Irina
Isabella
Katya (Ekaterina)
Lena (Elena)
Lenulia (Elena)
Liudmila (*Liusia*)
Liza (Elizaveta)
Liusia (Liudmila)
Marina
Manya (Maria)

Masha (Maria)
Nadya (Nadezhda)
Nastya (Anastasia)
Natasha (Natalia)
Nina
Olga
Raya (Raisa)
Rita
Svetlana
Tamara
Valeria
Varya (Varvara)
Vasilisa
Vera
Xenia
Zhanna
Zhenya (Evgeniya)
Zoya (Zinaida)

Masculine

(diminutive forms *italicized*)

Alexander (*Sasha*)
Alexey
Andrey
Boris
Borisovich (patronymic)
Danny (Danila)
Dmitry (*Mitya*)
Emelia (Emelian)
Evgeny
Feodor
Georgy
Grishka (Grigory)
Ippolit
Ivan (*Vanya, Vanechka, Ivanushka*)
Ivanushka (Ivan)
Khron
Kostya (Konstantin)
Kozma
Kuzma
Kuzmich (patronymic)
Lyonia (Leonid)
Martynka (Martyn)
Misha (Mikhail)

Mitya (Dmitry)
Nikita
Nikolay
Ostap
Pavel
Petr (*Petya*)
Petya (Petr)
Porfiry
Sasha (Alexander)
Semyon
Sergey
Slava
Tolya (Anatoly)
Vadim
Vasya (Vasily)
Victor (*Vitya, Vitka*)
Vitka (Victor)
Vladimir (*Vova*)
Vova (Vladimir)
Vseslav
Yegorych (patronymic)
Yuri

THE DOMINO MAN
Editor's afterword

In the spring of 2008 I retired to my farm in southern Montana. Having been through a long and turbulent career in book business, I did not plan to publish another book in my life!

Three months later I laid my hands on *this* book, and all my good intentions of slowing down were thrown out the window. But before committing to publishing this remarkable volume, I wanted to test it and see if it *really* worked—so I decided to try out "the magic" on a problem that was making me tense and restless.

Our farm was on a small gravel road not accessible by large trucks. So whenever I had some kind of freight coming my way—a piece of furniture, or a skid of books (I am still an avid reader)—I would arrange to meet the driver at a parking space at the intersecion of two rural highways. I would then squeeze the cargo into my van and haul it home.

The parking space where I met the trucks was surrounded by a lawn which was private property. The owner of the lawn, Bill, also owned a small convenience store across the road. The boundary between the public parking space and his private lawn was not fenced or demarkated in any way, so it was next to impossible to tell where one ended and the other began. This did not preclude Bill from feeling very particular about his property. When my huge trucks were arriving and turning into the parking area from the highway, sometimes they would go with one wheel over what he considered "his land."

Whenever that happened, he would leap out of his store and yell at us across the road: "Get off my land!" One time he even called county sheriffs on us, for trespassing.

Because of these experiences, I started feeling tense every time I expected a freight delivery, or even when I was driving by his store. But it is one thing to have a personal relationship issue, and quite another to be nervous about it and not sleep well the night before receiving a shipment.

I decided to apply the techniques described in this book. Searching for a *ray of light* was not difficult: I noticed how Bill especially enjoyed his social status. He was the owner of the store in the middle of very sparsely populated area, and his premises had naturally become a kind of a community center. Every night all the "real men" from the vicinity would come together at his store to play dominos. Bill would remain behind the counter, watching the game. He would invariably place his right hand on the counter, to show off a massive golden ring with a precious stone on it. He was, no doubt, counscious and proud of his special status in the community.

In my mind, I pictured this scenario: One night, the men are enjoying the usual game of dominos at Bill's store, while the owner proudly stands behind his counter. At the decisive moment of the game, Bill steps forward. He takes out of his pocket a domino, six-six, which begins expanding in his hand until it is the size of a concrete panel. He puts it crashing down on the playtable. The table collapses and the dominos shower down onto Bill's, which ends the game. He won, and all the other players look up at him in awe and amazement.

After this incident, the rumors start circulating that Bill is the best domino player in the world. Before long, his store sees a stream of visitors from all over the country and even overseas, coming to partake of his skill and wisdom. Eventually, in the place of his formerly inconspicuous store on the intersection of Montana's backroads, a highrise building is built—the World Domino Playing Academy. This highrise—glistening with white marble and dominating all surrounding landscape—is crowned with Bill's huge domino: six-six...

Arriving at the story's glorious end, I could no longer feel tense about the whole situation. Whenever I sensed the tension returning, I would bring the six-six domino back into my inner sight, and all worries would fall away.

In the "real" life, the situation was miraculously transformed. The trucks continued coming, and they would often go with one wheel over Bill's grass. But not a single time since then has he even walked out of his store.

A few days ago I passed by this intersection, only to see *three* large yellow trucks parked *on the grass* by the parking space, while Bill was riding his mower, mowing grass all around them. And although no skyscraper of white marble can be seen as yet, it is now apparently only a matter of time.

Leonid Sharashkin, Ph.D.

Ekalaka, Montana
August 1, 2009

We at Deep Snow Press *thank you* for reading this book and *offer you* an exclusive limited edition version of this remarkable volume, produced on the most environmentally sound paper ever—composed of 100% pressed snow. Offer valid while supplies of good humor last.

To discover other outstanding Deep Snow titles by Dolokhov & Gurangov and other authors, or to learn about upcoming gatherings and events, please visit us at

DEEP SNOW PRESS
www.DeepSnowPress.com

Refrigerate after opening.